Lush

LUSH

Recipes for the food you really want to eat

DANIEL LAMBERT

Ireland

This one's for you, Gaga

HarperCollinsIreland
The Watermarque Building
Ringsend Road
Dublin DO4 K7N3
Ireland

a division of
HarperCollinsPublishers
1 London Bridge Street
London SE1 9GF
UK

www.harpercollins.co.uk

First published by HarperCollinsIreland in 2022

1 3 5 7 9 10 8 6 4 2

Text © Daniel Lambert 2022
Photography © Leo Byrne 2022

Daniel Lambert asserts the moral right to be identified as the author of this work

A catalogue record of this book is available from the British Library

HB ISBN 978-0-00-852710-5

Designer: Graham Thew
Photographer: Leo Byrne
Food Stylists: Charlotte O'Connell and Clare Wilkinson

Printed and bound in Great Britain by
Bell & Bain Ltd

WHEN USING KITCHEN APPLIANCES PLEASE ALWAYS FOLLOW
THE MANUFACTURER'S INSTRUCTIONS

This book is produced from independently certified FSC™ paper
to ensure responsible forest management.

For more information visit: www.harpercollins.co.uk/green

CONTENTS

INTRODUCTION

My name is Daniel Lambert. I'm a professional fine dining chef, TikToker and occasionally I appear on your telly. This is my first cookbook and I'm thrilled that people like my recipes enough to want a book full of them!

If you follow me on TikTok or Instagram, you'll know that food makes me feel pretty emotional! I think food can make the world a better place, and all I want is to share the food that makes *me* incredibly happy with everybody else.

I was lucky enough to grow up in a family where everyone was amazing at cooking. My grandad was a chef most of his life – if he could see this book, it would definitely make him smile! I was always curious about food, and when I was about eight, my Auntie Crea taught me how to make a lasagne, step by step. That was my introduction to the world of cookery. Since then, experimenting with food and cooking for others has been a way for me to explore my creativity and get lost in my own little world.

I didn't always know I would be a chef. I failed my way through college because I had no interest in my course (and I may have been partying just a bit too much!). I tried working in marketing for a bit, but I didn't really enjoy that either. It was then that my Auntie Crea suggested culinary college. My family was so supportive and they encouraged me to pursue my love of cooking. My Nana Niamh even helped me get my first job in a kitchen, in a little café in Drumshanbo, where I got to learn the ropes. I owe her so much – and she still makes the best Bolognese in the whole world. During culinary school I got my first proper job in a professional kitchen. I took the opportunity to really hone my skills in the world of fine dining, learning from the expertise of the amazing chefs I got to work alongside. I even won some awards for my cooking, receiving gold medals in the Taste of Donegal competition three years in a row, and I was selected to compete in the final of the National Dairy Chef competition. But as much as I loved fine dining, in my spare time I kept getting creative with food, coming up with weird and wonderful flavour combos, copying my favourite takeaway dishes and always having fun and experimenting.

When COVID hit and the restaurant industry temporarily shut down, I suddenly had loads of free time. I decided to download TikTok and I was instantly hooked! One of the first videos I made was deep-fried Dorito-crusted cheese bites, and overnight it blew up, gaining over 1 million views. Next, a radio station contacted me and asked if I'd be interested in doing a series of recipes throughout Lockdown. In no time I was cooking on live television, appearing on *Ireland AM* and *Good Morning America*. It's been a crazy experience, and I've loved every minute of it. TikTok means I can reach people from all corners of the world with my food and I'm so lucky I get to do that. I love it when people try out my recipes and send me their pictures – it's the best feeling ever knowing one of my own creations is making someone on the other side of the planet happy.

I love fine dining, and I love the kind of food I make on my TikTok. Some people have said that it isn't 'real food', but as far as I'm concerned, there is no rulebook when it comes to cooking. Making lush, satisfying food that you really want to eat is so important. It's one of the greatest pleasures in life! So go ahead. Get stuck in, get creative and have fun. This is cooking, there are no rules.

CHEF'S NOTE: HOW TO

The key to following a recipe successfully is knowing a few basic techniques. This way your food will always be perfectly cooked and absolutely delicious!

HOW TO DEEP FRY

If you know me, you know my deep fat fryer is my best friend. If you make fried foods regularly, I recommend investing in a small deep fat fryer. They're easy to use and, because the oil is temperature controlled, it's safer than frying in a pot on the hob. Always follow the instructions that came with your deep fat fryer to achieve the best results.

If you don't have a deep fat fryer though, here are some tips on how to deep fry on the hob as safely as possible.

- Always use an oil with a high smoke point, such as sunflower or vegetable oil.
- Use a deep pot and enough oil so you can submerge a small batch of your food completely, but **never** fill it more than half full. Ideally it should be about one-third full and the walls of the pot should rise at least 10cm above the oil. This prevents the oil from spilling over and contains any oil spatters too.
- Preheat the oil to the cooking temperature. Use a probe or sugar thermometer held in the centre of the pot of oil to check the temperature. For consistent results, cook in small batches and let food come up to room temperature before frying it. Allow the oil temperature to heat back up between batches, as adding food will cool it down.
- Moisture can cause oil to spit, so gently pat foods dry with kitchen paper before adding to the oil.
- Don't get too close to the oil. Use long metal tongs or a slotted deep-frying spoon to insert and remove foods. Be gentle when inserting foods to avoid oil spatter.
- To prevent the food having a greasy taste or texture, drain it on kitchen paper after removing from the oil. You can gently pat food dry with kitchen paper to remove additional excess oil.

HOW TO SHALLOW FRY

Shallow frying is also called pan frying. When you fill a shallow pan with oil and heat it up enough that it sizzles when the food is added, you're shallow frying. Shallow frying uses less oil than deep frying and is a bit easier to manage, but still gives you a nice crispy result, so it's great for battered or breaded foods. Here are some tips for getting the best results when you shallow fry:

- Use a heavy-bottomed pan with sides that are at least 5cm high.
- For shallow frying, you want your oil to reach about 190°C. Use your probe or sugar thermometer to check.
- Don't crowd the pan, as the temperature of the oil will drop too much. If you're frying several batches, you can keep the already fried food warm in a low oven (about 90°C) while you work.
- Be sure to let food brown properly before flipping to get the best crispy finish possible.

If you time it right, you should only need to flip your food once.

- Like with deep-frying, drain food on kitchen paper as soon as it comes out of the pan to remove excess oil.

HOW TO PANÉ

'Pané' is just the cheffy name for coating food in flour, then egg, then breadcrumbs. You'll see this method in the book a lot, because we love breaded food. You will need three clean, shallow bowls or trays: one for the flour, one for the beaten egg and one for the breadcrumbs.

- First, put the food in the flour, making sure that it is well coated.
- Shake off any excess flour and put the food into the beaten egg, again making sure it is well coated.
- Shake off any excess and finally put the food into the breadcrumbs.
- Tap the food firmly to ensure that the breadcrumbs are well attached and remove from the crumbs onto a clean plate or tray. You can store panéd food in the fridge until you are ready to cook if you're not doing it right away.

I suggest that you use one hand for the flour and beaten egg and the other for the breadcrumbs, or you'll end up with fingers that look like chicken nuggets!

HOW TO MARINATE

The purpose of marinating is to add flavour to meat, fish or even veggies. It can also help tenderise the meat and stop it drying out when you cook it.

- The food you are marinating should be completely covered in the marinade. A great way to do this is to put your marinating meat into a sealable freezer bag and turn it over halfway through. Or use a bowl covered with plastic wrap, stirring the food halfway through the marinating time.
- Generally, the longer you leave your marinade on, the more flavour the food will absorb, but try to marinate for a minimum of 1 hour.
- Marinate your food in the fridge to prevent bacteria from developing.
- Leftover marinade is not safe to use as a sauce due to the exposure to raw meat, so it should be discarded.

Potato
Party

Ah, potatoes. If you've seen my TikTok, you know potatoes bring me endless joy. In my opinion, they're probably the most emotional food of all time. It amazes me how something so simple and affordable can be so versatile. There's just so much you can do with them.

In this chapter I've combined the absolute classics, like emotional roast potatoes and triple-cooked chips, with some weird and wonderful new inventions, like my cheesy potato doughnuts and nacho average baked potato. Once you've mastered mash and refined your fries, you can really get creative with your spuds. You could eat potatoes for dinner every day and never have the same meal twice. Isn't that mad?

Welcome to the land of spuds – if you're Irish, you're already home.

A Masterclass in Perfect Mashed Potato

Mash is seriously underrated. It's ideal when you need a serious feed and it goes well with everything. Unfortunately, perfect, sexy mash is hard to find – it's often lumpy, bland and under seasoned, and we don't want that. This recipe is a *mash*terclass in perfect mash that will leave you feeling satisfied every time.

Serves 4

— 6 large Maris Piper potatoes, peeled and roughly cut into 3cm chunks (see the chef's note)
— 2 litres vegetable stock, cooled
— 300ml cream
— 50g butter
— 300ml milk
— a small bunch of thyme
— salt and ground white pepper

To serve
— a knob of butter
— sea salt
— fresh thyme leaves

1 Place the potatoes and cold vegetable stock in a large pot and bring to the boil. Cook on a high heat until a butter knife easily slides through the spuds, about 20 minutes. Strain the potatoes using a colander and return them to the pot.

2 Put the cream, butter, milk and thyme into a small pot over a medium heat. You want to heat this just until the butter has melted and the mixture is starting to simmer. Do NOT let it boil! Turn off the heat and leave your cream mixture to infuse for a few minutes, then remove and discard the thyme.

3 Pour the cream mixture over the hot potatoes and mash with a potato masher or ricer. Season to taste with salt and ground white pepper, then serve with butter, sea salt and some fresh thyme leaves sprinkled over.

4 This is amazing served with the horseradish roast beef (page 41) or slow-cooked bacon and cabbage (page 34).

CHEF'S NOTE: Cutting the potatoes into evenly sized pieces makes them cook at the same rate. If you don't have a potato ricer but you like your mash extra smooth, you can pass it through a sieve at the end.

Emotional Roast Potatoes

Don't judge me, but I love roast potatoes so much, I sometimes wake up in the middle of the night craving them. I had the idea to try roasting the potatoes in a cupcake tin, and it was one of the best ideas I've ever had – it means each potato gets just the right amount of heat and oil so they get super crispy on the outside while staying fluffy on the inside. These are sure to make you feel emotional while you're eating your Sunday roast – or if you're like me, at 4 a.m. when the craving hits.

Serves 2–4 as part of a slap-up Sunday dinner

— 3 large Maris Piper potatoes, peeled and cut into quarters
— 1.5 litres vegetable stock, cooled
— vegetable oil
— salt and freshly ground black pepper

To serve
— fresh rosemary leaves

1 Preheat the oven to 200°C.
2 Place the potatoes into a large pot with the cold vegetable stock and bring to the boil. Simmer for 2 minutes then strain, return them to the empty pot and allow them to steam dry. This increases the starch content and gives you those amazing fluffy insides!
3 Put a teaspoon of vegetable oil in each cup of a 12-cup metal cupcake tin, then place the tray in the preheated oven for 15 minutes to get the oil really hot.
4 Remove the cupcake tray and place one piece of spud in each cup. Be careful here as the oil will be insanely hot! Turn the oven down to 170°C and roast the potatoes for 25–30 minutes, turning them every 10 minutes or so. Keep an eye on them as they may need more or less time depending on your oven. When they're golden brown and crispy, they're ready!
5 Sprinkle over some fresh rosemary, season to taste with salt and black pepper and enjoy!

CHEF'S NOTE: If you don't have a metal cupcake tray, you can use a regular roasting tin. Just put in 65ml of oil and heat in the oven as above before roasting.

Irish Hash Browns

Hash browns are a classic American breakfast food, but I like to soak my potatoes in Guinness for added flavour and Irishness. I mean, Guinness and spuds, it doesn't get any more Irish than that, does it? These are just what you need when you're craving something carby and comforting. As they need an hour in the freezer before frying, you'll need to get these going an hour before you want to eat them.

Serves 4

— 6 large Maris Piper potatoes, peeled
— 250ml Guinness (from a can)
— 1 litre vegetable stock, cooled
— 1 tablespoon cornflour
— 1 teaspoon salt, plus extra for seasoning
— ½ teaspoon ground white pepper
— 1 litre vegetable oil

To serve
— coarse sea salt

1 Line a baking sheet with baking paper. Put the spuds in a large pot with the Guinness and cold vegetable stock. Bring it the boil and cook for 2 minutes, then strain the potatoes using a colander and allow them to go cold – if you try to do the next step while the potatoes are still hot you'll just end up with a disaster. Good things come to those who wait, my friend!

2 Coarsely grate the potatoes into a large bowl. Add the cornflour, salt and pepper and mix it all together. For each hash brown, use about 3 heaped tablespoons of the mixture and mould it to your desired shape. I like to press the potato mix into a circular cutter first, then use my hands to pat them into an oval shape.

3 Place your patties on the lined baking tray and freeze for about an hour.

4 Pour enough oil into your frying pan to come to about 5mm up the side (approximately 300ml depending on the size of your frying pan). Heat the oil over a medium heat until it's starting to shimmer. You can test it by adding a small cube of bread – if the bread starts to sizzle, your oil is ready. Add your hash browns and fry until golden brown, about 2 minutes each side. Remove to your lined baking sheets and sprinkle with a little coarse sea salt before serving, if you like.

To-die-for Fries Two Ways

I don't discriminate – I love fries in all shapes and forms. Chunky, skinny, sweet, spicy, it's all good!

Here are two ways you can make fries at home depending on your mood – very different, but equally delicious.

Sticky Sweet Potato Fries

I came up with this recipe after I went out for dinner one evening and the restaurant had completely sold out of sweet potato fries! I came home still craving them, so I got into the kitchen and got to work. I think you'll agree these are even better than anything you could order out.

Serves 4

— 2 litres vegetable stock, hot
— 5 sweet potatoes (about 1kg), washed and cut into skinny chips
— 1-2 litres vegetable oil
— 200g honey
— 1 teaspoon chilli flakes
— 1 teaspoon salt
— 1 teaspoon garlic powder

1 Line two baking sheets with kitchen paper.
2 Bring the vegetable stock to the boil in a large pot. Add your sweet potato chips and boil for 2 minutes. Strain the chips, return to the pot and leave to steam dry.
3 Heat the oil in your deep fat fryer to 140°C – you will need about 2 litres depending on the size of your fryer. If you don't have a deep fat fryer, you'll need a thermometer or temperature probe, a deep saucepan and about a litre of vegetable oil – your pot should be no more than one-third full.
4 Fry the chips for 5 minutes, then remove to your lined baking sheets. Allow the chips to cool for a few minutes, then turn the heat up so the oil reaches 180°C and return the chips to the fryer. Cook until golden brown and crispy, about another 5 minutes. When they're ready, transfer the chips back to the lined baking sheets.
5 For that glorious sticky sauce, put the honey, chilli flakes, salt and garlic powder in a frying pan and bring to a gentle simmer over a medium heat. When it's sticky and bubbling, add in the chips and toss gently with a spatula to coat them.

CHEF'S NOTE: If you prefer your chips chunky, simply cut the sweet potatoes into larger slices and boil for an extra 2 minutes.

Triple-cooked Chips

Life is too short to be eating soggy potatoes. That's why I always cook my chips three times for maximum crispiness.

Serves 4

— 2 litres vegetable stock, hot
— 5 Maris Piper potatoes, peeled and cut into skinny chips
— 1–2 litres vegetable oil
— sea salt

1 Line two baking sheets with kitchen paper.

2 Bring the stock to the boil in a large pot. Add your chips and boil for 2 minutes. Strain the chips and return them to the pot, letting them steam dry so they're nice and fluffy.

3 Heat the oil in your deep fat fryer to 140°C – you will need about 2 litres depending on the size of your fryer. If you don't have a deep fat fryer, you'll need a thermometer or temperature probe, a deep saucepan and about a litre of vegetable oil – your pot should be no more than one-third full.

4 Fry the chips for 5 minutes, then remove to your lined baking trays. Allow the chips to cool for a few minutes, then turn the heat up so the oil reaches 180°C and return the chips to the fryer. Cook until golden brown and crispy, about another 5 minutes.

5 When they're ready, transfer the chips to the lined baking sheets. Season generously with sea salt and serve.

Cheesy Potato Doughnuts

This recipe came about when I was sitting at home craving doughnuts, but also in the mood for something savoury ... and so the cheesy potato doughnut was born! These are amazing – the buffalo mozzarella filling gives you the most incredible cheese pulls and the polenta coating brings the crunch factor. There are a lot of steps to this one but believe me when I say they're worth the effort!

Makes 6

— 6 Maris Piper potatoes, peeled and cut into quarters
— 2 litres vegetable stock, cold
— 50g butter, melted
— 100ml cream
— salt and freshly ground black pepper
— 1 teaspoon vegetable oil
— 3 shallots, chopped
— 1 teaspoon fresh thyme leaves
— ½ tablespoon finely chopped fresh parsley, plus extra to serve
— 2 x 150g buffalo mozzarella balls, drained
— 100g plain flour
— 3 eggs, beaten with a splash of milk
— 200g polenta or semolina

1 Line a baking sheet with baking paper.
2 Place the potatoes and cold vegetable stock in a large pot and bring to the boil. Cook on a high heat until a butter knife easily slides through the spuds, about 20 minutes. Strain the potatoes and put them back in the pot.
3 Mash the potatoes with a masher or put them through a potato ricer. Add the melted butter, cream and salt and pepper to taste and mix together with a wooden spoon.
4 Heat the teaspoon of vegetable oil in a frying pan and fry the shallots and thyme over a medium heat for 2 minutes, until the shallots are just starting to soften. Fold the shallots and parsley into your potato mix.
5 To make your doughnuts, cut each of the mozzarella balls into three pieces so you have six pieces of cheese. Divide the potato mixture into six portions and use your hands to shape each portion into a flat patty. Press a piece of cheese into the centre of each patty and mould the potato around this to form a ball. Place all the doughnuts onto your lined baking sheet and freeze for about half an hour, until firm.
6 Heat the oil in your deep fat fryer to 170°C. You will need about 2 litres depending on the size of your fryer. If you don't have a deep fat fryer, you'll need a thermometer or temperature probe, a deep saucepan and about a litre of vegetable oil – your pot should be no more than one-third full.
7 Put the flour, beaten eggs and polenta or semolina into three shallow bowls. Coat the doughnuts by dipping them in the flour first, then the egg and finally the polenta/semolina. Deep fry them for 2 minutes on each side, until golden brown, then serve with some fresh parsley scattered over.

CHEF'S NOTE: You can also use panko breadcrumbs to coat the doughnuts.

Nacho Average Baked Potato

These are 'nacho' average baked potato – see what I did there? I crack myself up sometimes. If you know me, you know I love to fuse my favourite foods together to make weird and wonderful mash-ups. This combo of crispy baked potato and fully loaded nachos is an absolute winner – perfect to line the stomach before you head out for the night or for a chilly Friday night in front of the telly.

Makes 4

— 4 large rooster potatoes, well scrubbed
— 4 tablespoons extra virgin olive oil
— salt and freshly ground black pepper
— 1 tablespoon vegetable oil
— 500g minced beef
— 1 tablespoon ground cumin
— 1 tablespoon paprika
— 1 tablespoon garlic powder
— 200ml beef stock
— 50g tomato paste
— 100g tomatoes, chopped
— 150g tortilla chips
— 200g mozzarella cheese, grated

To serve
— sour cream
— 4 spring onions, finely sliced

1 Preheat your oven to 170°C.

2 Place the potatoes in a baking dish or on a baking sheet. Cut an X in the top of each potato, then pour over the olive oil and season generously with salt and pepper.

3 Wrap each spud in tin foil and bake in the preheated oven for 1 hour. While they're baking, you can get on with making your mince.

4 Heat the vegetable oil in a frying pan. Add the minced beef, cumin, paprika and garlic powder and fry, stirring regularly, until the beef is brown. Add in the beef stock, tomato paste and chopped tomatoes and simmer on a medium heat for about 20 minutes, stirring occasionally, until the sauce is nice and thick.

5 After about 50 minutes, check that your potatoes are cooked through by sticking a butter knife into them. It should slide in easily. Pull them slightly apart at the top where you cut them and stick the tortilla chips into them as shown in the picture. Scoop the mince on top, then sprinkle over the mozzarella and place under a preheated grill until the cheese is bubbly and golden brown. Top with dollops of sour cream and spring onions and dig in!

Irish Boxty Pancakes

If you haven't had boxty before, you are in for a treat. It's a traditional Irish pancake made with two types of potato: grated and mashed. These are a great way to use up leftover mashed potatoes (see page 8) – if you're lucky enough to have leftovers! These make an amazing breakfast, but they're great for dinner, too.

Makes 10

— 200g potatoes, peeled
— 200g leftover mashed potato
— 180g plain flour
— 220ml buttermilk
— salt and freshly ground black pepper
— 1 tablespoon vegetable oil
— 1 tablespoon butter

1 Preheat your oven to 180°C and line a baking sheet with baking paper.

2 Start by coarsely grating the raw potatoes into a large bowl. Next, you need to get all the excess water out of the potato by tipping it all onto a clean tea towel, gathering up the corners to make a little bundle and squeezing this out over the sink.

3 Put the grated potato, leftover mash and flour into a large bowl and mix until well combined. Add in the buttermilk and salt and pepper to taste, and stir until your mixture has the consistency of lumpy pancake batter.

4 Heat the vegetable oil and butter in a frying pan until sizzling. Scoop 2 heaped tablespoons of batter into the pan for each pancake. Fry the boxty pancakes for 2 minutes on each side, until golden brown, then transfer to your baking sheet. When all the batter has been used up – you should have about 10 pancakes – put your baking sheet in the preheated oven and finish the pancakes off by baking for 5 minutes.

CHEF'S NOTE: You can really get creative with the toppings for these bad boys – think cheese and ham, crispy bacon and maple syrup, sour cream and spring onion …

Irish-style Potato Nachos

I always knew these would be a hit on TikTok, and they were – everyone loved the idea of turning potatoes into nachos! This is the ultimate in fusion cuisine.

Serves 6

For the nacho mince
— 1 tablespoon olive oil
— 500g Irish beef mince (8% fat is best)
— 200g smoked bacon, diced
— 1 onion, diced
— 300ml Guinness
— 100ml beef stock
— 150g tomatoes, chopped
— a sprig of thyme
— 2 tablespoons Worcestershire sauce
— 1 teaspoon ground cumin
— 1 teaspoon cayenne pepper
— 1 teaspoon garlic powder
— 1 teaspoon paprika
— 1 teaspoon onion powder
— 1 teaspoon brown sugar
— salt

For the potato slices
— 6 large Maris Piper potatoes, scrubbed
— 1–2 litres vegetable oil

To serve
— 150g Cheddar cheese, grated
— sour cream
— 4 spring onions, finely sliced

1 Start by heating the olive oil in a frying pan. Add the beef mince and bacon pieces and fry over a medium heat, stirring regularly, until the mince is brown and the bacon is cooked. Add the onion into the pan and cook for a further minute or so.

2 Pour the Guinness into the pan. Let this reduce for about 10 minutes on a medium heat. Once the stout has reduced, add in the beef stock, chopped tomatoes, thyme, Worcestershire sauce, spices and sugar. Stir until everything is combined, season well with salt and let the nacho mince simmer gently for about 20 minutes, until it has thickened nicely.

3 Cut your potatoes lengthways into 5mm-thick discs and pat them dry with a clean tea towel or kitchen paper.

4 Heat the oil in your deep fat fryer to 180°C – you will need about 2 litres depending on the size of your fryer. If you don't have a deep fat fryer, you'll need a thermometer or temperature probe, a deep saucepan and about a litre of vegetable oil – your pot should be no more than one-third full.

5 Fry the potatoes for 8–10 minutes, until golden brown and crispy. Season them with salt and place in a single layer on a baking tray lined with baking paper.

6 Once your mince mix is ready, spoon it on top of your potatoes. Try to work fast or you risk your spuds starting to get soggy! Sprinkle the grated Cheddar over the mince and place under a medium-high grill until the cheese is golden brown.

7 Transfer the nachos to a serving dish, if you like – I usually just eat these straight from the tray! Top with dollops of sour cream and spring onions. Serve immediately.

CHEF'S NOTE: You can really play with the toppings on these – try adding guacamole, sliced red jalapeños, tomato salsa, refried beans ... The possibilities are endless.

The Perfect
Crisps

For me, crisps are the king of snacks – the perfect thing to munch on a Friday night in watching a film. This recipe will show you how to make the crispiest ones you'll ever have, better than anything you could get in the shop.

Makes 4 servings

— **4 large Maris Piper spuds, peeled and thinly sliced with a mandolin or vegetable peeler**
— **white wine vinegar**
— **1-2 litres vegetable oil**
— **sea salt**

1 Line two baking sheets with kitchen paper.
2 Put the potato slices in a large bowl, pour over enough vinegar to cover and allow to soak for at least an hour.
3 Remove the potato slices from the vinegar and dry them well using a clean tea towel or kitchen paper. Heat the oil in your deep fat frier to 180°C. You will need about 2 litres depending on the size of your fryer. If you don't have a deep fat fryer, you'll need a thermometer or temperature probe, a deep saucepan and about a litre of vegetable oil – your pot should be no more than one-third full.
4 Deep fry the potato slices for 6 minutes, until golden and crispy. Transfer the crisps to the lined baking sheets and leave them to cool to room temperature. Season generously with sea salt and enjoy!

CHEF'S NOTE: FLAVOUR VARIATIONS
If you're a fan of salt and vinegar flavour, mix together 1 teaspoon salt and ½ teaspoon vinegar. Leave the salt to infuse overnight then sprinkle it over your crisps.

You can also try soaking the potato slices in Guinness instead of vinegar to make the most unreal Guinness-flavoured crisps.

The Potato Hoagie Wrap

There's nothing better than coming home from the pub and demolishing a kebab. This potato hoagie wrap is similar to a kebab, but it swaps out the lamb or chicken for golden, crispy fried potato cubes. This is all you need to fill the gap when you're at your most peckish, perfect day or night.

Makes 4

— 1-2 litres vegetable oil
— 3 large Maris Piper potatoes, peeled and cut into evenly sized cubes
— 1 tablespoon vegetable oil
— 4 tablespoons ground cumin
— 2 tablespoons garlic powder

To serve
— 4 large tortilla wraps
— 4 tablespoons sour cream
— 2 tomatoes, diced
— 4 spring onions, thinly sliced
— 50g Parmesan cheese, grated
— salt and freshly ground black pepper
— 1 tablespoon butter (optional)

1 Line a baking sheet with kitchen paper. Heat the oil in your deep fat fryer to 150°C – you will need about 2 litres depending on the size of your fryer. If you don't have a deep fat fryer, you'll need a thermometer or temperature probe, a deep saucepan and about a litre of vegetable oil – your pot should be no more than one-third full.

2 Fry the spuds for 5 minutes, then turn the heat up so the oil reaches 180°C and continue frying until golden brown and crispy, another 4–5 minutes.

3 In a frying pan heat the tablespoon of vegetable oil and add the cumin and garlic powder. Toss the spuds in the spice mixture until the spices smell gorgeous and fragrant – this is called 'cooking off' and usually takes about 5 minutes. If you don't cook off spices they can leave a nasty burning sensation in your throat!

4 To assemble the wraps, warm the tortillas by microwaving on high power for 20 seconds. Top each wrap with some potato cubes, then dress it up with the toppings of your choice. I love this with sour cream, tomatoes, spring onions and Parmesan cheese, all seasoned with salt and pepper, but you could also use grated Cheddar cheese, tomato salsa, guacamole, barbecue sauce, crispy fried onions – whatever you fancy. Go nuts!

5 Fold the wraps and they're ready – or if you want to toast them, melt the butter in a frying pan and fry the wraps on both sides until they are a light golden brown.

Summer BBQ Potato Salad

I never show up to a barbecue without plenty of this; it's always a huge hit. This salad is perfect on a hot day and goes with chicken, burgers, pork chops – anything, really.

Serves 8-10 as a side

— 10 Maris Piper potatoes, peeled and cut into evenly sized chunks
— 200g smoked bacon lardons
— 1 teaspoon vegetable oil
— 5 tablespoons good-quality mayonnaise
— 2 teaspoons white wine vinegar
— 7 spring onions, finely sliced
— salt and freshly ground black pepper

1 Place the potatoes in a large pot, cover with cold water and bring to the boil. Cook on a high heat until a butter knife easily slides through the spuds. Strain using a colander and allow to cool.

2 Fry the bacon in the oil until nice and crispy. Put to one side while you make the dressing.

3 For the salad dressing, whisk the mayonnaise and white wine vinegar together in a jug. Put the potatoes, spring onions and cooled bacon in a bowl, pour over the dressing and stir with a wooden spoon until combined, mashing the potatoes lightly with the back of the spoon for a creamier texture, if you like. Season to taste with salt and pepper and serve.

Trad
Fest

This is food to make your granny happy – it's wholesome, warming and nostalgic. I don't know about you, but there's something about a plate of bacon and cabbage that just takes me back to my childhood. If you didn't feel patriotic enough after the potato party, you've come to the right place.

Just because food is traditional doesn't mean it has to be boring. I'm always experimenting in the kitchen and this chapter is no different. I've taken classic soda bread and added rosemary, lemon and honey to make the perfect loaf for dipping in soup. If you want to seriously impress the family, my roast beef has a horseradish crust that makes it extra juicy and gives it a bit of a kick – try serving it up with the most seductive side ever, my boozy Cointreau-glazed carrots. Fair warning, though – you'll probably be asked to host Sunday dinner for the rest of your life.

Rosemary and Lemon Soda Bread

Soda bread always cheers me up. It's such a cosy comfort food – perfect with soup on a Sunday evening or toasted for breakfast on a cold winter morning. Here I've taken a classic Irish soda bread recipe and jazzed it up a bit with lemon, honey and rosemary.

Makes 1 loaf

- 260g wholemeal flour
- 180g plain flour
- 1 teaspoon bicarbonate of soda
- 1 teaspoon salt
- 360ml buttermilk
- 1 large free-range egg
- 1 tablespoon honey
- 1 tablespoon lemon zest
- juice of 1 lemon

1 Preheat your oven to 180°C and line a baking sheet with baking paper.

2 Sieve the two flours, the bicarbonate of soda and the salt into a large mixing bowl.

3 Whisk the remaining ingredients together in a jug, then make a well in your dry ingredients and slowly pour the wet ingredients in, using a wooden spoon to mix as you go. This ensures everything gets evenly incorporated so there are no lumps.

4 When you have a smooth, soft dough, dust a clean surface with a handful of plain flour and tip the dough out. Knead the dough for 1 minute, until it's no longer sticky, then shape into a large round.

5 Use a knife to lightly score an X into the top of the dough, transfer to the baking sheet and bake in your preheated oven for 30–40 minutes, until nicely browned all over. Leave to cool before slicing.

CHEF'S NOTE: Bread is tricky because it's different every time you make it! If you find your dough is too wet and sticky, add some extra flour. If it's too dry, add a splash of water.

Slow-cooked Bacon and Cabbage

Here's a meal that is guaranteed to impress your granny. I know it looks like there's a lot of steps in there, but stay calm – the slow cooker makes the bacon and cabbage a doddle, and once you get the hang of making parsley sauce it's dead easy. Give it a try for Saint Patrick's Day to impress the family.

Serves 4

For the bacon and cabbage
— 50g runny honey
— 50g wholegrain mustard
— freshly ground black pepper
— 1kg bacon loin
— whole cloves (optional)
— 1 star anise
— 1 head of savoy cabbage, stems removed and leaves finely chopped

For the parsley sauce
— 25g butter
— 25g plain flour
— 600ml milk
— 1 tablespoon finely chopped fresh parsley
— salt and freshly ground black pepper

To serve
— mashed potato (page 8)

1 In a small bowl, mix the honey and mustard together with a few generous grinds of black pepper. Use a sharp knife to score the fat on your bacon loin and massage the marinade into the bacon. You can stick some cloves into the fat for extra flavour, if you like.

2 Put the bacon in your slow cooker with the star anise. Cook on a high heat for 4½ hours, then add in your chopped cabbage and cook for another 30 minutes.

3 While your cabbage is cooking you can get on with making your parsley sauce. Melt the butter in a medium-sized pot, then add in the flour and cook, stirring constantly, over a medium heat until the mixture forms a stiff paste, about 2 minutes. This is called a roux and it's the base for your white sauce. Congratulations, you're basically a chef now!

4 Take your roux off the heat and place it on a heatproof surface. Gently heat the milk in a separate pot until it's steaming. Slowly pour the milk into the roux, whisking with the other hand the whole time, until it's all evenly incorporated with no lumps. Cook the white sauce over a low heat, stirring continuously, until it has thickened enough to coat the back of a wooden spoon – about 8 minutes. Take it off the heat, stir in the parsley and season with salt and pepper to taste.

5 Preheat the oven to 180°C.

6 Remove the bacon from the slow cooker and transfer it to a roasting tin. Roast for 10 minutes until gorgeous and golden. Allow the bacon to rest for a few minutes before slicing – it should be perfectly tender.

7 For a seriously impressive-looking plate, pour a small amount of the parsley sauce on the plate, top with a generous spoonful of cabbage and a few slices of juicy bacon, then dollop some mash beside it. And there you have it, a beautiful Saint Patrick's Day dinner.

CHEF'S NOTE: I've made the white sauce here from scratch, but if you're short on time you can buy a jar of white sauce from any major supermarket and jazz it up by warming it in a pot and stirring in your chopped parsley and some freshly ground black pepper. Sure nobody has to know.

Potato Bread (Boxty)

If you haven't had a big slice of this with a full Irish, you haven't lived, my friends. This is amazing for soaking up your baked beans or try buttering two slices and using it to make the most emotional sausage sambo imaginable.

Makes 10–12 large slices

— 500g mashed potatoes
— 10 large Maris Piper potatoes, peeled
— 4 shallots, finely diced
— 4 sprigs fresh thyme, leaves picked
— 1 tablespoon vegetable oil
— 150g plain flour
— ½ tablespoon baking powder
— salt and freshly ground black pepper
— 500ml buttermilk

1 Preheat your oven to 180°C and line a baking sheet with parchment paper.

2 This is a great way to use up any leftover mash, but if you're making it from scratch, follow the instructions on page 8, then allow your mash to cool to room temperature. Coarsely grate the raw potatoes into a large bowl. Get all the excess water out of the potato by tipping it all onto a clean tea towel, gathering up the corners to make a little bundle and squeezing this out over the sink.

3 Fry the shallots and thyme in the vegetable oil over a medium heat until the shallots have softened, about 8 minutes.

4 Sift the flour, baking powder, salt and pepper into a large mixing bowl, then add the mashed potato, buttermilk, grated potato and cooled shallots. Mix everything together with a wooden spoon – you should end up with a wet dough.

5 Spread the mix all over the lined baking sheet with a spatula or wooden spoon and bake in the oven for 40 minutes, until golden brown. Allow to cool to room temperature before slicing and serving.

CHEF'S NOTE: If you want to make this gluten free, swap out the plain flour for any gluten-free flour blend.

Cabbage Crisps

These are a genuinely addictive snack, but if you want to be fancy you can also add them to your dishes to feel like a real chef. Be careful when frying these because the oil will spit – I recommend wearing some gloves and standing well back!

Makes 6 servings

— 1 head of green leafy cabbage
— 1-2 litres vegetable oil
— sea salt

1 Line two baking sheets with kitchen paper.
2 Rinse the cabbage and discard the outer leaves. Peel the remaining leaves from the stalk and dry them thoroughly with kitchen paper – this step is important because water and deep frying just don't mix! Cut the cabbage leaves into large strips.
3 Heat the oil in your deep fat fryer to 180°C – you will need about 2 litres depending on the size of your fryer. If you don't have a deep fat fryer, you'll need a thermometer or temperature probe, a deep saucepan and about a litre of vegetable oil – your pot should be no more than one-third full.
4 Deep fry the cabbage leaves in batches for 1-2 minutes, until crispy. Transfer the leaves to the lined baking sheets and allow to cool. Season to taste with sea salt and enjoy.

Horseradish Roast Beef

You'll be the most beloved person in your house if you start making this one on Sunday afternoons – the smell of this when the oven door opens could wake the dead. Don't skip out on the horseradish sauce – it not only adds flavour, but it creates a kind of crust on the beef, keeping it super juicy.

Serves 6

— 1.5kg silverside of beef
— 1 carrot, peeled and roughly chopped
— 1 onion, roughly chopped
— 1 celery stick, roughly chopped
— 1 bulb of garlic, separated but not peeled
— a few sprigsof thyme, leaves picked
— olive oil
— salt and freshly ground black pepper
— 2 tablespoons horseradish sauce
— 1 tablespoon vegetable oil

1 Take the beef out of the fridge to come to room temperature an hour before you want to use it.
2 Preheat the oven to 200°C.
3 Place the prepared veggies, garlic cloves and the thyme leaves in a roasting tin. Drizzle over some olive oil, sprinkle with salt and pepper and toss to coat. Spread the horseradish sauce over the beef using a spoon or a pastry brush and season lightly with salt. Sit the beef on top of the veggies in the roasting tin.
4 Cook in the oven for 1 hour for medium or about 50 minutes for medium rare. Flip the beef over halfway through cooking – this makes the juices run down through the meat and keeps it gorgeously tender.
5 Remove the beef from the oven to a warmed plate and lightly cover it with tin foil. Allow to rest for 15 minutes or so before transferring to a chopping board and slicing.

CHEF'S NOTE: The juices from the beef give you the most amazing base for the Guinness gravy on page 45, and they're a match made in heaven.

The Best Guinness Gravy

Left alone with this gravy, I could probably drink it. I think gravy turns a regular roast into something really special, and this is absolutely made for the horseradish roast beef (see page 41). Homemade gravy usually takes hours to make, but I've come up with a really handy shortcut so you can have this on the table in no time.

Serves 6 with the horseradish roast beef

— 2 teaspoons vegetable oil
— 1 onion, roughly chopped
— 1 stick of celery, roughly chopped
— 1 leek, roughly chopped
— 4 cloves of garlic, chopped
— 5 black peppercorns
— 5 sprigs of thyme
— 250ml Guinness
— 1 litre beef stock
— meat juices from the roast beef (optional)
— 1 tablespoon beef gravy granules
— salt and freshly ground black pepper

1 Heat the vegetable oil in a very large pot. Add the vegetables, garlic, peppercorns and thyme and fry for 2 minutes just to bring the flavour out. Pour in the Guinness and cook until it has reduced by half, about 10 minutes. Add in the stock and meat juices, if using, and bring to the boil. Simmer for a further 15–20 minutes, until everything is reduced by half.
2 Strain the gravy into a clean pot and discard the vegetables. Return the gravy to the heat, then add in the gravy granules and stir until it reaches your preferred thickness (see the chef's note for more details). Season to taste with salt and pepper and serve.

CHEF'S NOTE: You can adjust the thickness of the gravy to get it just the way you like it by adding more gravy granules to thicken or an extra drop of water or beef stock to thin it out.

Honey and Cointreau Glazed Carrots

I bet you never knew carrots could be the star of the show, did you? These are the bomb – make them at Christmas and watch your family's eyes just light up. I never thought a vegetable could make me emotional, but I'll be honest, these carrots do it for me.

Serves 6

— 6 carrots, peeled and chopped on the diagonal into chunks
— 50ml honey
— 25ml Cointreau
— 1 star anise
— 25ml white wine vinegar
— 5 black peppercorns

1 Bring a large pot of salted water to the boil, add your carrots and boil for about 3 minutes, until just getting soft.
2 Put all remaining ingredients in a large frying pan and cook over a medium heat, whisking once it starts to bubble. When the sauce is sticky, add in the carrots and continue to cook for another minute, until they're really shiny.

Potato and Leek Soup

This is a hug in a mug right here. I'm not a doctor, but I reckon this will cure whatever ails you. Give it a go and warm your belly.

Serves 4–6

— 2 teaspoons vegetable oil
— 10g butter
— 100g smoked bacon, chopped
— 4 large potatoes, peeled and cut into chunks
— 1 small carrot, peeled and diced
— 1 small onion, diced
— 1 small stick of celery, diced
— 2 leeks, sliced
— 2 cloves of garlic, chopped
— 1 teaspoon salt
— 1.5 litres vegetable stock
— leaves from 1 sprig of thyme
— 125g baby spinach
— 250ml cream, plus extra for serving
— 250ml milk
— salt and ground black pepper

1 Put the oil and butter in a large pot over a medium heat. When the butter is melted and beginning to foam, add in the bacon and fry until crispy. Use a slotted spoon to scoop the bacon out and set aside for later. Leave all that bacon fat in the pan – this will give your soup the most amazing savoury flavour.
2 Throw all the vegetables and garlic in the pan with the salt. Fry for 10 minutes, until they're just starting to soften, then add the vegetable stock and thyme. Simmer this on a low heat for 30–40 minutes, stirring occasionally, until the vegetable mix is meltingly tender.
3 Just before you're ready to serve, throw in the spinach, cream and milk, take the pot off the heat and blitz with a stick blender until smooth. Season to taste with salt and pepper, then ladle into bowls or mugs and top with an extra swirl of cream and the reserved crispy bacon bits.

CHEF'S NOTE: When my nan makes this, she leaves out the milk, cream and spinach and serves it chunky – it's great either way, but however you make it, you definitely need to serve this with the Guinness bread on page 115.

So Wrong but So Right

Bacon and banana, coffee and cheese, curry and pasta... No, I haven't lost the plot. In this chapter we're taking ingredients that really don't sound like they belong together and pairing them up to make some of the most delicious and addictive creations you've ever tasted.

This is proof that being creative pays off. Can't decide between Italian and Chinese food? My slow-cooked chicken curry lasagne will tick all your boxes. Ever put Red Bull on your chicken wings? You don't know what you're missing out on! And you might think I'm truly mental for suggesting spreading mayo all over your cheese toastie, but you'll just have to trust me here. When these weird and wonderful combos work, they really work.

Brace yourself – these recipes will satisfy cravings you never even knew you had...

Slow-cooked Chicken Curry Lasagne

I know, I know – chicken curry lasagne sounds a bit mental, but the more I imagined the comforting flavours of a classic chicken curry combined with the cheesy, starchy goodness of a lasagne, the more I knew I had to make it happen. Try it and I think you'll agree this is a match made in comfort food heaven.

Serves 4

— 4 chicken breasts, cut into chunks
— 3 tablespoons medium curry powder
— ½ teaspoon salt
— 1 pepper, finely diced
— 1 onion, finely diced
— 750ml chicken stock
— 1 x 400g tin of chopped tomatoes
— 200ml coconut milk (½ a tin)
— 12 lasagne sheets
— 200g mozzarella cheese slices

1 Put the chicken pieces into a bowl and toss with 1½ tablespoons of the curry powder and the salt until they are well coated. Throw the chicken, vegetables and remaining curry powder into your slow cooker. Add the stock, chopped tomatoes and coconut milk, stir until everything is combined and cook on low for 4 hours.
2 Once your filling is ready, preheat your oven to 180°C.
3 It's time to assemble your lasagne. Place a layer of lasagne sheets in a family-size baking dish, then top with a third of your filling, then top with mozzarella slices. Repeat until all your filling is used up, finishing with a layer of cheese.
4 Bake in the oven for 35–40 minutes, until the pasta is soft and the cheese is bubbly and golden.

Boozy Wings
Two Ways

Imagine all the flavours of a night out, but in a piece of chicken … that's what I did anyway, and I came up with these mad, boozy wing recipes that work way better than they should. Trust me – grab your mates, get them round to the gaff and make these this weekend. You'll thank me later.

Jäger Bomb Chicken Wings

Serves 4

— 1kg chicken wings
— 500ml buttermilk
— 1–2 litres vegetable oil
— 2 tablespoons plain flour
— 2 tablespoons Jägermeister
— 150ml Red Bull
— 3 tablespoons barbecue sauce

To serve
— spring onions, sliced
— sour cream and chive dip
  (page 185)

1 Line a couple of baking sheets with kitchen paper. Put the wings in a bowl, pour enough buttermilk over to cover them, and leave to soak for at least an hour or up to 8 hours in the fridge. Remove the wings from the buttermilk and place in a bowl with the flour. Toss to coat.

2 Heat the oil in your deep fat fryer to 180°C – you will need about 2 litres depending on the size of your fryer. If you don't have a deep fat fryer, you'll need a thermometer or temperature probe, a deep saucepan and about a litre of vegetable oil – your pot should be no more than one-third full.

3 Fry the wings in batches for 5 minutes, until they're crispy all over, then transfer to your lined baking sheets.

4 Put the Jägermeister and Red Bull into a large frying pan over a medium heat. Once it's starting to bubble, add in the barbecue sauce. Add in the wings and toss them in the sauce to coat.

5 Scatter some spring onions over and serve with sour cream and chive dip.

Buckfast Chicken Wings

Serves 4

— 1kg chicken wings
— 2 tablespoons plain flour
— 1 tablespoon paprika
— 1–2 litres vegetable oil
— 500ml Buckfast
— 3 tablespoons barbecue sauce
— 1 tablespoon sesame seeds
— a handful of fresh coriander, chopped

1 Line a couple of baking sheets with kitchen paper. In a bowl, toss the chicken wings with the flour and paprika until coated.

2 Heat the oil in your deep fat fryer to 180°C – you will need about 2 litres depending on the size of your fryer. If you don't have a deep fat fryer, you'll need a thermometer or temperature probe, a deep saucepan and about a litre of vegetable oil – your pot should be no more than one-third full.

3 Fry the wings in batches for 5 minutes, until they're crispy all over, then transfer to your lined baking sheets.

4 Heat a large frying pan or wok until it starts to smoke, then pour in the Buckfast, standing well back. It should start sizzling straight away. Reduce this by half, then add in the barbecue sauce and whisk together. Once the mixture is nice and sticky, throw in the chicken wings and sesame seeds and stir until the wings are completed coated in the sauce.

5 Scatter over the freshly chopped coriander and serve.

Coca-Cola Slow-cooked Ribs

The combination of salty ribs, sweet cola and sticky barbecue here is just perfect – better than anything you could get from your local Chinese takeaway. I highly recommend a pile of egg fried rice or some of the triple-cooked chips on page 15 to serve with these bad boys.

Serves 4–6

— 250ml Coca-Cola
— 1 teaspoon black peppercorns
— zest and juice of 1 orange
— 200g barbecue sauce
— 1kg pork ribs
— salt and freshly ground black pepper

1 Start by making the sauce. Put the Coca-Cola, peppercorns, orange zest and juice in a pot and bring to the boil. Simmer until the mixture has reduced by half, then add the barbecue sauce and whisk everything together. You should have a nice sticky glaze.
2 Season the ribs with plenty of salt and black pepper. Pour half the sauce into the slow cooker, add the ribs, then pour over the remainder of the sauce. Cook for 2 hours on a high heat, then reduce to low for another 2 hours.
3 Finish the ribs off under a medium-high grill for 2 minutes if you like them extra crispy!

Coca-Cola Ham

Strange as it may sound, this isn't a new idea – people have been cooking ham in Coca-Cola for years. There's a good reason for it too, as the sweetness of the Coke really balances out the saltiness of the ham and the acidity is a great meat tenderiser. It's the perfect addition to Christmas dinner and you can have a bit of fun asking people to guess what that flavour is!

Serves 4–6

— 1kg ham fillet

For the brine
For every 2 litres of water used:
— 1 cinnamon stick
— 2 star anise
— 2 teaspoons pink peppercorns
— 1 bay leaf
— 1 tablespoon sugar

For the glaze
— 1 x 330ml can of Coca-Cola
— 2 teaspoons wholegrain mustard
— 2 star anise
— a sprig of rosemary
— 6 cloves
— 2 teaspoons Worcestershire sauce

1 Make up enough of the brine mix to cover your ham and let it soak in the fridge overnight. I usually do this in a large mixing bowl or pot and cover it with a lid or cling film.
2 The next day, when you're ready to cook, make up the glaze by mixing all the ingredients together in a jug. Put the ham in your slow cooker and pour over the prepared glaze. Cover and cook on a low heat for 6 hours. It should be really tender and starting to fall apart at this stage.
3 Preheat your oven to 200°C.
4 Transfer the ham to a large roasting tin and reglaze it with the juices left over in the bowl of the slow cooker. Roast for 5–10 minutes, until the glaze is bubbling. Slice and enjoy!

CHEF'S NOTE: If you have any of this left over, add it to the ultimate mayo three-cheese toastie (see page 71) for a serious upgrade.

Vegetable Spring Rolls with Sticky Club Orange Sauce

If you've never made your own spring rolls before, you'll be amazed at how easy it is to whip these up. You can get frozen filo pastry in most big supermarkets – I suggest keeping a stash of it in your freezer for when you get a craving for these (and once you've tried them, you definitely will). Using Club Orange, or any other fizzy orange, gives you an amazing sauce with classic Chinese sweet-and-sour flavours. Heaven.

Makes 20 spring rolls

For the dipping sauce
— 1 x 330ml can of Club Orange or Fanta
— 1 tablespoon white wine vinegar
— 1 teaspoon black peppercorns
— 1 star anise
— 1 tablespoon sugar

For the spring rolls
— 1 tablespoon sesame oil, plus extra for brushing
— 1 small carrot, peeled and cut into thin strips
— ½ head of Chinese cabbage, shredded
— 1 white onion, finely chopped
— 1 garlic clove, minced
— 3 spring onions, sliced
— 2 tablespoons soy sauce
— 1 tablespoon white wine vinegar
— salt and ground white pepper
— 1 x 270g packet of frozen filo pastry, defrosted

1 Preheat the oven to 180°C.

2 Put all the sauce ingredients in a frying pan and bring to the boil. Simmer until the Club Orange is reduced by half and the sauce is starting to get nice and sticky. Strain the sauce and set aside for later.

3 Heat the sesame oil in a frying pan and stir fry the carrot and cabbage over a high heat for 3 minutes, then add in the onion, garlic and spring onions and cook for another 2 minutes. Add the soy sauce and vinegar and continue to stir fry until the veggies become nice and soft, then let them cool. Season to taste with salt and white pepper.

4 On a chopping board, cut the filo pastry into even squares about 15cm x 15cm. To roll, take a square of pastry and turn it so it looks like a diamond. Place a spoonful of veggies in the centre of the diamond. Using a pastry brush, lightly wet the outside corners with a small amount of water, then fold in the left and right points so they meet in the middle. Now tightly roll the pastry from the bottom up, and you have a spring roll!

5 Pop the spring rolls on a non-stick baking sheet, brush with sesame oil and bake them in the preheated oven for 10–12 minutes, until golden brown. Pass around a bowl of the sticky sauce for dipping.

CHEF'S NOTE: If your sauce still isn't thick enough when it's cooled, here's an easy fix. Dissolve 1 teaspoon of cornflour in 2 teaspoons water. Bring the sauce to a simmer and add the cornflour mixture. Stir and cook for another minute or so – the sauce should thicken really quickly. You can use this trick to thicken almost any kind of sauce or gravy.

Pizza Pasta Bake

Arriving home one night after a long day in work, I really fancied a pizza but I also felt like having some pasta, and now look what we have here – the best of both worlds! I'll never go back to choosing between them again.

Serves 2

— 200g tagliatelle
— 2 tablespoons olive oil
— 50g tomato paste
— 50g cherry tomatoes
— 170g cream cheese
— a few fresh basil leaves, chopped
— salt and freshly ground black pepper

For the toppings
— pepperoni slices
— 1 ball of buffalo mozzarella, sliced
— a few fresh basil leaves

1 Preheat the oven to 180°C.
2 Cook the tagliatelle in salted boiling water for the time given on the packet, then drain and set aside while you make the sauce.
3 Heat the olive oil in a frying pan. Add the tomato paste and cook for a couple of minutes over a medium heat, then add the cherry tomatoes and cook until they're starting to soften. Add the cream cheese and basil and simmer gently until you have a lovely thick sauce.
4 Pour the sauce into a round baking dish. Add the cooked pasta to the dish and mix well to combine with the sauce. Season to taste with salt and pepper.
5 Here's the fun bit. Top the pasta with as much pepperoni and mozzarella as you like. Sprinkle with black pepper and bake in the preheated oven until the cheese is bubbly and golden brown. Use a spatula to remove the pasta bake to a plate and scatter with fresh basil leaves before serving.

Cheeseburger Tacos

Anything that involves a bit of DIY at the dinner table is good craic, and this is perfect for a movie night when the whole family is at home. Don't skip the emotional sauce, it's the ultimate burger sauce and really takes these to the next level.

Makes 4

— 4 large sesame-seeded burger buns
— 1 tablespoon vegetable oil
— 400g lean beef mince
— 1 tablespoon ground cumin
— ½ tablespoon paprika
— 1 teaspoon cayenne pepper
— ½ teaspoon salt
— a generous pinch of freshly ground black pepper

To serve
— emotional sauce (page 190)
— 1 head of iceberg lettuce, finely shredded
— American-style cheese slices
— pickle slices
— spring onions, finely sliced
— 1 small white onion, very finely diced

1 Flatten out the burger buns with a rolling pin – these will be your taco shells. Set aside for later.
2 Heat the vegetable oil in a frying pan. Add the beef mince, spices and salt and pepper and cook until the beef is brown and most of the moisture has evaporated.
3 While the beef is cooking, make the emotional sauce, following the recipe on page 190, and assemble all your toppings.
4 To serve, I like to put the beef and toppings out on the table with the burger bun tacos and let everyone serve themselves.

Coffee and Cheese Arancini

You've probably never seen coffee and cheese together on an ingredients list before, but don't judge this until you try it – they are amazing together. An arancini is basically a ball of cold risotto, breadcrumbed and deep-fried until crispy and golden brown – it's classic Italian street food and it tastes unreal.

Serves 4–6

— 2 tablespoons olive oil
— 300g Arborio rice
— 3 cloves of garlic, minced
— 3 shallots, finely diced
— 250ml white wine
— 500ml black coffee
— 1 litre vegetable stock, hot
— 200g Parmesan cheese, grated, plus extra to serve
— a pinch of sea salt
— 100g plain flour
— 3 eggs, beaten with a splash of milk
— 200g panko breadcrumbs
— 1–2 litres vegetable oil

1 Heat the olive oil in a large, heavy-based pan, add the rice and fry for 2 minutes, until it starts to smell nutty – that means the rice is nicely toasted. Add in the garlic and shallots and cook for a further 2 minutes.

2 Pour in the white wine and stir to deglaze the pan. Once the wine has been almost completely absorbed, add in the coffee. Simmer, stirring continuously, until the coffee has reduced by half. Now start to add in the vegetable stock. It's best to do this slowly – I add a cupful of stock at a time and stir until each cup has been absorbed before I add more – and keep stirring so the rice doesn't stick. When all the liquid has been absorbed, add the Parmesan cheese and the salt and stir to combine. Congrats, you've made a risotto!

3 Remove the risotto from the heat to cool to room temperature and line a baking sheet with baking paper. Take scoops of the mix and roll them into balls about the size of golf balls. I find it easier to do this if I wet my hands with a little bit of cold water first. Put the balls on the lined tray and freeze them for 1 hour, until firm.

4 Put the flour, beaten eggs and panko breadcrumbs into three shallow bowls. Coat the balls by dipping them first in the flour, then the egg and finally the panko.

5 Heat the oil in your deep fat fryer to 180°C – you will need about 2 litres depending on the size of your fryer. If you don't have a deep fat fryer, you'll need a thermometer or temperature probe, a deep saucepan and about a litre of vegetable oil – your pot should be no more than one-third full.

6 Deep fry the arancini for 3 minutes, until golden brown all over, then transfer to a plate lined with kitchen paper. Serve topped with a sprinkle of freshly grated Parmesan.

Pizza in a Pineapple

Now this one will definitely divide people. Personally I think pineapple on pizza is amazing, but why stop there? Why not put pizza *inside* a pineapple? This looks really fun and it tastes great. In fact, one of my Instagram followers loved this idea so much, they asked their local pizza place to recreate it for them!

Serves 2

— 1 large pineapple, sliced in half lengthways
— 1 x 400g tin of chopped tomatoes
— 2 cloves of garlic, chopped
— 1 teaspoon chilli flakes, plus more to top
— 50g granulated sugar
— leaves from a small bunch of fresh basil
— salt and freshly ground black pepper
— 200g mozzarella cheese, grated
— 75g pepperoni slices

1 Start by preparing your pineapple. Remove the flesh from both halves of the pineapple, leaving a 2cm-thick shell. Cut the pineapple flesh into bite-sized cubes and place these back inside the two pineapple halves.

2 For the sauce, bring the tomatoes, garlic, chilli flakes and sugar to a simmer in a saucepan. Cook for 10 minutes, add the basil leaves and then remove from the heat. Add salt and pepper to taste, then blend with a stick blender or in a food processer until smooth.

3 Spoon the sauce over the pineapple in its shells, then top with the cheese and pepperoni and scatter some chilli flakes over, depending on how spicy you want it. Place under a grill on a medium-high heat until the cheese is golden brown and bubbling, then dig in.

The Ultimate Mayo Three-cheese Toastie

Cheese toasties are a thing of beauty. But how can you improve on perfection? I'll tell you – slather it in mayonnaise and stuff it with three types of cheese.

Makes 1

— 2 slices of white sourdough bread
— 1 tablespoon mayonnaise
— 20g white Cheddar cheese, grated
— 20g mozzarella cheese, grated
— 10g red Cheddar cheese, grated
— freshly ground black pepper

To serve
— extra mayonnaise
— ketchup

1 Spread the mayo on both slices of bread, front and back – trust me.

2 Assemble by topping the first slice of bread with the three cheeses and a generous sprinkle of freshly ground black pepper. Top with the second slice of bread. Good job, you have successfully made a sambo.

3 Fry the sandwich in a dry frying pan on a very low heat for 5 minutes on each side – the oil in the mayo will make it gorgeously crispy and golden. When the cheese starts to ooze, it's ready. Serve with some extra mayo and ketchup for dipping.

The
Cure

Let's face it, we all know the feeling of a rough day after a particularly heavy night out on the sesh. If you wake up with a sore head and a dry mouth, craving something comforting that you can put together with just the ingredients you have in your kitchen, you've come to the right place. Nurse your hangover and fill your belly with dorito mozzarella sticks and loaded fries, or have a fakeaway feast with a homemade chicken fillet roll or sausage and egg muffin.

Frying Pan Pizza

Proper homemade pizza is amazing, but it takes a long time to make from scratch. This quick and easy frying pan pizza is the perfect way to satisfy your cravings in less than the time it would take to get one delivered.

Makes 4

— 250g plain flour
— 150ml warm water
— 1 teaspoon salt
— 2 tablespoons vegetable oil

For the toppings
— 200g passata
— 200g grated mozzarella
— 100g salami or pepperoni slices (optional)

To serve
— 1 fresh red chilli, deseeded and sliced
— fresh basil leaves
— freshly grated Parmesan

1 Mix the flour, water, salt and vegetable oil together in a mixing bowl and knead on a lightly floured surface until the dough is smooth. Let this rest for 1 hour in the fridge.

2 Cut the dough into four even pieces. Roll each piece out as thinly as possible, into approximately 20cm circles – these will be your pizza bases.

3 Cook the pizza bases on a dry frying pan one at a time. Fry on a medium to high heat until air bubbles starts to form, about 2 minutes, then flip and cook for another 2 minutes.

4 Spread each pizza with passata, top with mozzarella, then add salami or pepperoni (if using). Place the pizzas under a grill and cook until the cheese is melted and bubbling, about 5 minutes. Sprinkle with some fresh chilli slices, fresh basil and freshly grated Parmesan.

CHEF'S NOTE: For that real fakeaway feeling, serve this with garlic mayo (page 181).

Pork Belly Ramen Noodle Bowl

I love anything that has a savoury, umami flavour like this dish. My ramen noodle bowl is a comforting Japanese-style wonder that will leave you with a full belly. You can change up the toppings to suit your own taste too – try adding finely sliced chilli, bamboo shoots, fresh coriander, bean sprouts or even some strips of nori seaweed.

Serves 4

— sesame oil
— 300g pork belly, cut into even strips
— 4 spring onions, finely sliced
— 200ml light soy sauce
— 2 eggs
— 100g chestnut mushrooms, sliced
— 150ml dark soy sauce
— 1 litre chicken stock
— 50g fresh sweetcorn
— 1 tablespoon sesame seeds, toasted in a dry frying pan, plus extra to serve
— 400g ramen noodles
— 1 pak choi, sliced

1 Heat 1 tablespoon of sesame oil in a large frying pan and sear the pork belly over a high heat until browned all over.

2 Add half the spring onions and the light soy sauce and cook, stirring, until the pork belly is cooked through and the sauce is sticky. Take off the heat and leave to one side for now.

3 Bring a small pot of water to a boil, add the eggs and time them for 5 minutes. While the eggs are boiling, fill a bowl big enough to cover the eggs with water and a handful of ice cubes. When the eggs are ready, carefully remove them from the boiling water and place in the bowl of ice water for 1 minute. This prevents the eggs cooking further once removed from the hot pot. Peel the eggs and slice them in half.

4 In a large pot, heat a drizzle of sesame oil. Fry the mushrooms for 2 minutes over a high heat, then add in the dark soy sauce, chicken stock, sweetcorn and toasted sesame seeds. This is your broth.

5 Cook the ramen noodles in this broth following the packet instructions. Add the pak choi and cook for 30 seconds. Ladle the noodles and broth into four bowls, then top with the pork belly, a halved egg, the reserved sliced spring onions and more sesame seeds.

Instant Noodle Wrap

Yes, this is a bit different, but bear with me. There's nothing better than carbs on carbs when you're feeling a bit fragile, and dipped into some chicken soup, this is brought to a whole other level. Pure, filthy goodness.

Makes 4

— **4 packets of your favourite instant noodles**
— **4 tortilla wraps**
— **200g mozzarella cheese, grated**
— **a generous knob of butter**

1 Cook the noodles according to the packet instructions, then drain and add the noodle seasonings.

2 Warm the tortilla wraps in the microwave for 20 seconds. Divide the noodles between the wraps and top with cheese. Fold the wraps by bringing in the edges and then rolling up like a burrito.

3 Melt some butter in a frying pan and fry the wraps for 2 minutes on each side, until the wraps are crispy and golden and the cheese is melted.

Hangover Wedges

I was lying in bed one morning, starving, dehydrated, head pounding ... and all I had in the press was a bag of spuds and a few spices. I was too hungover to go to the shops, so I decided to whip up some wedges with what I had. It turned out to be one of my best inventions yet.

Serves 4

— 8 Maris Piper potatoes, unpeeled and cut into wedges
— 2 litres vegetable stock, cooled
— 100g runny honey
— 1 tablespoon paprika
— 1 tablespoon garlic powder
— 1 tablespoon onion powder
— 1 tablespoon cayenne pepper
— 2 teaspoons olive oil
— zest and juice of 1 lime
— ½ teaspoon salt

To serve
— garlic mayo (page 181)

1 Place your potatoes and cold vegetable stock in a large pot and bring to the boil. Cook over a high heat until you can pierce the wedges with a fork.
2 Preheat the oven to 180°C.
3 Strain the wedges and tip them out onto a large baking tray lined with baking paper. Let them cool down for a few minutes so you don't burn your hands doing the next bit.
4 In a small bowl or jug, whisk together the honey, paprika, garlic powder, onion powder, cayenne pepper, olive oil, lime zest and juice and salt. Drizzle this mixture over the wedges and use your hands to toss them so they're evenly coated. Bake in the preheated oven for 25–30 minutes, until nice and crispy.
5 Serve with the garlic mayo.

Super Nachos

This is your sign to invite your mates round for a nacho night. I promise if you whip these up, everybody will love you. Nachos are a great choice for a group DIY dinner – just load up the table with plenty of toppings and let everyone dress theirs up just the way they like.

Serves 2-4, depending on how hungry you are

- olive oil
- 500g beef mince (8% fat)
- 200g smoked bacon, chopped
- 1 onion, diced
- 100ml beef stock
- 150g tinned chopped tomatoes
- 2 tablespoons Worcestershire sauce
- salt
- 1 teaspoon cayenne pepper
- 1 teaspoon garlic powder
- 1 teaspoon paprika
- 1 teaspoon onion powder
- 1 teaspoon ground cumin
- 1 x 200g bag of tortilla chips
- 150g Cheddar cheese, finely grated

To serve
- 100g sour cream
- 100g guacamole (shop bought is fine)
- 2 spring onions, sliced
- 1 red jalepeño, finely sliced (optional)

1 Heat a small drizzle of olive oil in a hot pan, then add your minced beef. Stir, then add in your diced smoked bacon pieces. Once the beef and bacon are nicely browned and cooked, add the onion into the pan, and stir to mix.

2 After 1 minute, add in the beef stock, followed by the tomatoes, Worcestershire sauce and salt. Now add the cayenne pepper, garlic powder, paprika and onion powder. Let your nacho mince simmer for 20 minutes, stirring occasionally, until it thickens nicely.

3 Once the mince is ready, spread out your tortilla chips on a large ovenproof plate or dish. Spoon the nacho mince on top, then sprinkle the cheese over and grill until the cheese is melting and slightly browned.

4 Top with the sour cream, guacamole, spring onions, and jalapeños if you like. Put the plate in the middle of the table and let everyone tuck in!

Dorito Mozzarella Sticks

These mozzarella sticks bring two of my favourite foods together in a single snack. Believe it or not, this is also the recipe that launched my TikTok career!

Makes 12

— 2 x 125g balls of mozzarella cheese
— 100g plain flour
— 3 eggs, beaten with a splash of milk
— 200g Doritos (whatever flavour you like), crushed

1 Preheat the oven to 180°C. Line a baking sheet with baking paper.
2 Start by cutting the mozzarella balls into sticks. Slice each ball in half, then cut each half into three sticks.
3 Put the flour, beaten eggs and crushed Doritos in three shallow bowls. Dip the cheese sticks in the flour, then the egg and then in the crushed Doritos.
4 Transfer the mozzarella sticks to the baking sheet and cook in the preheated oven for 5–10 minutes, until crispy and golden.

Cheese and Chorizo Potato Bites

This snack is inspired by a tapas dish that I order whenever I eat out in a Spanish restaurant. You'll have to trust me on this, but I think the homemade version is even nicer.

Serves 4-6

— 100g chorizo, finely diced
— olive oil
— 300g mashed potato
— 200g mozzarella cheese, diced
— salt and freshly ground black pepper
— 1–2 litres vegetable oil
— 100g plain flour
— 3 eggs, beaten
— 200g panko breadcrumbs

1 Line a baking sheet with baking paper. You can use leftover mash for this, but if you're making it from scratch, follow the instructions on page 8, then allow your mash to cool to room temperature.

2 Fry the chorizo in a lightly oiled frying pan until it gets crispy, then remove from the frying pan with a slotted spoon and allow to cool. Mix the chorizo, mashed potato, mozzarella, salt and black pepper together in a bowl.

3 Roll the mixture into golf ball-sized rounds, place on your lined baking sheet and freeze for about 30 minutes, until firm.

4 Place the flour, eggs and panko breadcrumbs in three shallow bowls. Coat the potato bites by dipping them first in the flour, then the egg and finally the breadcrumbs.

5 Heat the oil in your deep fat fryer to 170°C – you will need about 2 litres depending on the size of your fryer. If you don't have a deep fat fryer, you'll need a thermometer or temperature probe, a deep saucepan and about a litre of vegetable oil – your pot should be no more than one-third full.

6 Deep fry the bites until golden brown, about 2 minutes on each side. Remove to a plate or baking sheet lined with kitchen paper and allow to cool slightly before serving.

Loaded Fries
Two Ways

How do you make fries even better?
Easy, just load them up! Try topping
yours with my emotional cheese sauce,
or with all the best bits of a Full Irish.
Either way, make a double batch
because I guarantee you'll eat more
than you expect.

Full Irish Fries

Serves 4

— 1 portion of triple-cooked chips
  (page 15)
— vegetable oil
— 4 sausages
— 4 slices of smoked bacon
— 4 slices of white pudding
— 4 slices of black pudding

To serve
— tomato ketchup

1 First get your chips on: follow the instructions to
make the triple-cooked chips on page 15.
2 Heat a drizzle of vegetable oil in your frying pan. Fry
the sausages over a medium heat until cooked through,
then turn the heat up to high, add the bacon and the
white and black puddings and fry until everything is
crispy.
3 Roughly chop the sausages, bacon and puddings and
serve over the fries with loads of tomato ketchup.

Emotional Cheese Fries

Serves 4

— 500ml milk
— 1 small onion, peeled and studded
  with cloves
— 25g butter
— 25g plain flour
— 1 teaspoon ground cumin
— 300g white Cheddar cheese, grated
— salt and freshly ground pepper
— 1 portion of triple-cooked chips
  (page 15)

1 Start by infusing your milk with flavour by gently heating it in a saucepan with the clove-studded onion for a few minutes. Turn off the heat, remove the onion, then leave the milk to one side for now.

2 Melt the butter in a separate pan, then stir in the flour and cook for about 2 minutes, until you have a paste (this is called a roux). Gradually add in the warm milk, whisking constantly to avoid lumps forming. Add in the cumin and grated cheese and whisk everything together over a low heat until the sauce has thickened – about 5 minutes. Season to taste with salt and pepper.

3 Follow the instructions to make the triple-cooked chips on page 15. Plate the chips, pour over as much cheese sauce as you like, and serve.

CHEF'S NOTE: The cheese sauce will thicken as it cools – reheat it gently in a saucepan before pouring it over the chips if you need to.

Sausage and Egg Muffin

I love a good McDonald's fakeaway, and if you ask me, with the homemade sausage patties, this is even nicer than the real thing.

Makes 4

— 300g pork mince
— ½ teaspoon ground white pepper
— ½ teaspoon salt
— 2 tablespoons butter
— 4 eggs
— 4 English muffins
— 4 slices of your favourite cheese

To serve
— emotional sauce (page 190)
— smoked bacon jam (page 198)
— hot sauce

1 Mix the pork mince, white pepper and salt together in a bowl and shape into four patties. If you have a ring mould, you can use that to shape your patties, but if not just use your hands.

2 Fry the sausage patties in half the butter on a medium heat until browned on both sides and cooked through, then remove to a warm plate nearby.

3 Melt the rest of the butter in the same pan and crack in your eggs. Use ring moulds if you have them to get the perfect round shape. I like to start the eggs on a low heat, then turn up to a high heat, add a tablespoon of water to the pan and cover with a lid so the eggs steam.

4 Split and toast your muffins under a grill or in a toaster. Top each muffin with a slice of cheese, sausage patty and egg and serve with emotional sauce or smoked bacon jam and a drizzle of your favourite hot sauce.

Chicken Fillet Rolls

Possibly the greatest Irish hangover feed of all time: the chicken fillet roll. But if trekking to your local petrol station to get one of these when you're absolutely dying isn't your idea of a good time, this recipe is the answer.

Makes 4

— 4 chicken breasts
— 500ml buttermilk
— 100g plain flour
— 3 eggs, beaten with a splash of milk
— 100g fresh breadcrumbs, mixed with
  ¼ teaspoon black pepper

To serve
— 4 small baguettes
— garlic mayo (page 181)
— shredded iceberg lettuce
— 1 small red onion, finely diced

1 Put the chicken breasts into a bowl, pour over the buttermilk and marinate in the fridge for at least 1 hour or up to 24 hours – the longer you marinate, the more tender the chicken will be.

2 Preheat the oven to 180°C and line a baking sheet with baking paper.

3 Put the flour, beaten eggs and breadcrumbs in three separate bowls. Dip the chicken in the flour, eggs, then the breadcrumbs, arrange on the baking sheet and bake in your preheated oven for 12–15 minutes, until golden and crispy. Allow to cool for a few minutes, then slice.

4 To assemble your chicken fillet roll, split the baguettes and spread with some garlic mayo. Top with sliced chicken breast, lettuce and red onion and enjoy.

BBQ Beef Ranchero Tacos

If you're craving something smoky and spicy this is exactly what you need. The Jack Daniels BBQ sauce adds a touch of sweetness. I love serving this in a taco but the mince also makes a great topping for chips or wedges.

Serves 4-6

— 700g beef mince
— 2 onions, diced
— 1 teaspoon yellow mustard powder
— 1 tablespoon ground cumin
— 1 teaspoon onion powder
— 1 teaspoon chilli powder
— 200g sweetcorn
— 200g red kidney beans, from a tin

To serve
— Jack Daniels BBQ sauce (page 196)
— 12 soft corn tortillas warmed
— sour cream
— grated cheddar cheese
— shredded baby gem lettuce
— salsa

1 Brown off your mince in a hot saucepan or skillet, then add your onions and cook them until soft in the juice and fat that is in the pan from your beef. Add in the spices and cook, stirring, for about 4 minutes. Throw in your sweetcorn and kidney beans and cook for a further 3 minutes on a low heat. Set aside while you make the BBQ sauce on page 196.
2 Spread as much BBQ sauce as you like on the warmed tortillas, then fill with beef and top with sour cream, cheese, baby gem lettuce and your favourite salsa.

CHEF'S NOTE: If you have time, it's definitely worth making the Jack Daniels BBQ sauce for serving – but if you're in a hurry, just use a big dollop of your favourite shop-bought BBQ sauce.

Smoked Bacon Beef Burgers

There's nothing more disappointing than slapping a shop-bought burger on the barbecue and watching it shrink as it cooks. This recipe is the solution – these burgers are juicy with a really good bite to them, they pack serious flavour, and they won't shrivel up on the grill!

Makes 4

— 500g beef mince
— 150g smoked bacon lardons
— 2 eggs, beaten
— 100g breadcrumbs
— 1 tablespoon American mustard
— 1 tablespoon tomato ketchup
— 2 cloves of garlic, minced
— fresh thyme, leaves picked and chopped to make 2 teaspoons
— 1 shallot, finely chopped
— salt and freshly ground black pepper

To serve
— Jack Daniels BBQ sauce (page 196)
— shredded iceberg lettuce
— 1 red onion, thinly sliced
— 4 slices of Cheddar cheese
— 8 rashers of smoked bacon, fried until crispy
— 4 burger buns, toasted

1 Mix all the ingredients for the burgers together in a large mixing bowl and season with salt and pepper. Mould into four burger patties with your hands.
2 Cook the burgers on a barbecue or on a frying pan over a medium-high heat, turning every few minutes, until the burgers are fully cooked all the way through – this should take about 12 minutes.
3 Assemble your burgers by layering up the BBQ sauce sauce, lettuce, onions, burgers, cheese and bacon on the bottom bun, then place the other bun on top and devour.

Jambons

Nobody has time to make pastry from scratch first thing in the morning, but everybody has time to turn a sheet of shop-bought puff pastry into these delicious homemade jambons. You won't believe how easy it is to put these together.

Makes 6

— 500ml milk
— 25g butter
— 25g plain flour
— 100g white Cheddar, grated
— 200g smoked bacon lardons, cooked
— salt and freshly ground black pepper
— 1 x 375g pack of ready-rolled puff pastry sheets
— egg wash (made by whisking an egg with a little milk)

1 Preheat the oven to 200°C. Line a baking sheet with baking paper.

2 Heat the milk in a saucepan and set aside. Melt the butter in a separate saucepan, then stir in the flour and cook for about 2 minutes, until you have a paste (called a roux). Gradually add in the hot milk, whisking constantly to avoid lumps forming.

3 Add in the cheese, bacon and seasoning and whisk everything together over a low heat until the sauce has thickened – about 5 minutes. Season with salt and pepper, then leave this mixture to cool.

4 Cut the puff pastry into six even squares. Divide the mixture evenly between the squares, then fold the corners in so they touch in the middle, to make little parcels (see the photos on the opposite page). Brush with the egg wash, transfer to the baking sheet and cook in the preheated oven until golden and crispy.

Sausage Rolls

As much as I love a deli counter sausage roll, preferably bought at a petrol station and eaten sitting in my car, I think I might just love these homemade ones even more. Added bonus? Not getting pastry crumbs all over my car seat.

Makes 10

— 1 x 375g pack ready rolled puff pastry sheets
— 400g pork mince
— salt and freshly ground black pepper
— fresh thyme, leaves picked and chopped to make 2 teaspoons
— 2 eggs, beaten
— egg wash (made by whisking an egg with a little milk)

To serve
— ketchup

1 Preheat the oven to 200°C. Line a baking sheet with baking paper.
2 Unroll the sheet of puff pastry and cut it in half lengthwise to make two long rectangles. Lay out one rectangle of pastry on the baking sheet, with the long edge closest to you.
3 In a bowl, mix the pork mince with the salt, pepper and thyme, add in the eggs and mix everything together well. Take half of the filling and shape it into a long log shape down the middle of the first pastry rectangle. Ensure the meat is tight and compact, without gaps.
4 Brush one long edge of pastry with egg, then roll it up, sealing on the edge with the egg wash on it and finishing with the seam side down. Repeat the whole process with the other pastry rectangle and the remaining sausage mix.
5 Slice each roll into five and use the tip of a sharp knife to score the top of the pastry – this allows steam to escape and stops the sausage rolls from bursting open in the oven. Brush the tops of the rolls with the egg wash and bake in the preheated oven for 10–15 minutes. Serve with ketchup.

CHEF'S NOTE: If you have the time, refrigerate the pastry rolls for 1 hour before you slice them – it makes them easier to cut.

Battered Sausages

In my humble opinion, you get the best battered sausages in chippers in Dublin or on the north coast of Ireland. They're a favourite of mine so I've perfected the batter in this recipe – I promise you won't be disappointed.

Makes 6

— 10g baking powder
— 25g cornflour
— 200g plain flour, divided
— 1 teaspoon salt
— 1 tablespoon white wine vinegar
— 1 ice cube
— 6 sausages
— 1–2 litres vegetable oil
— flaky sea salt

1 Line a baking sheet with kitchen paper.

2 To make the batter, mix the baking powder, cornflour, 100g flour, salt and vinegar together in a bowl. Slowly add a little water, 1 tablespoon at a time, until your batter thickly coats the back of a spoon. Add the ice cube and leave the mix for 20 minutes, then give it a quick stir.

3 Put the remaining flour in a bowl, then dip the sausages in the remaining flour, then the batter.

4 Heat the oil in your deep fat fryer to 180°C – you will need about 2 litres depending on the size of your fryer. If you don't have a deep fat fryer, you'll need a thermometer or temperature probe, a deep saucepan and about a litre of vegetable oil – your pot should be no more than one-third full.

5 Deep fry the sausages in the oil for 5–8 minutes, until crispy. Transfer the battered sausages to the lined baking sheet and sprinkle with flaky salt before serving.

CHEF'S NOTE: You'll probably have plenty of batter left over, so use it for the battered beef burgers on the next page ... or make more sausages.

Battered Beef Burgers

These are another classic chipper menu item I can't get enough of. They're coated in the same batter as the battered sausages on page 102, so if you're feeling especially filthy, you could whip up a double batch and make a full-on chippie feast. Just don't forget the curry sauce to pour over!

Makes 4

— 500g beef mince
— 150g smoked bacon lardons
— 2 eggs, beaten
— 100g breadcrumbs
— 1 tablespoon American mustard
— 1 tablespoon tomato ketchup
— 2 cloves of garlic, minced
— fresh thyme, leaves picked and chopped to make 2 teaspoons
— 1 shallot, finely chopped
— 100g plain flour
— 1–2 litres vegetable oil

For the batter
— 100g plain flour
— 25g cornflour
— 10g baking powder
— 1 teaspoon salt, plus extra to serve
— 1 tablespoon white wine vinegar
— 1 ice cube

To serve
— flaky sea salt
— your favourite curry sauce

1 In a bowl, mix together all the burger ingredients except the flour and shape into burgers with a mould or with your hands. Don't make them too big or they won't cook properly in the fryer.

2 To make the batter, mix the flour, baking powder, cornflour, salt and vinegar together in a bowl. Slowly add a little water, 1 tablespoon at a time, until your batter thickly coats the back of a spoon. Add the ice cube and leave the mix for 20 minutes, then give it a quick stir.

3 Sear the burgers on a hot frying pan until they are brown all over. Put them to one side to cool and put the remaining flour in a bowl. Coat the burgers in the flour, then dip them in the batter.

4 Heat the oil in your deep fat fryer to 180°C – you will need about 2 litres depending on the size of your fryer. If you don't have a deep fat fryer, you'll need a thermometer or temperature probe, a deep saucepan and about a litre of vegetable oil – your pot should be no more than one-third full.

5 Deep fry the burgers in the oil for 5–8 minutes, until crispy. Transfer the battered burgers to a baking sheet lined with kitchen paper and sprinkle with flaky salt before serving with your favourite curry sauce.

Korean Chicken

This might just be the ultimate hangover cure. It's sticky and sweet and the gochujang paste gives it a real kick. Addictive stuff.

— 4 chicken breasts, sliced into long, thick strips
— 240ml buttermilk

For the crispy coating:
— 175g plain flour
— 1 teaspoon salt
— 1 teaspoon ground black pepper
— ½ teaspoon garlic powder
— 1 teaspoon paprika
— 1 teaspoon chilli flakes
— 1-2 litres vegetable oil, for frying

For the sauce:
— 2 tablespoons gochujang paste
— 2 tablespoons honey
— 4 tablespoons light brown sugar
— 4 tablespoons light soy sauce
— 2 cloves of garlic, peeled and minced
— 2 teaspoon ginger, grated
— 1 tablespoon sesame oil

To serve:
— 3 spring onions, sliced thinly
— 1 teaspoon sesame seeds

1. Place the chicken in a bowl. Add the buttermilk, cover and place in the fridge to marinate for at least 1 hour or up to overnight.

2 When you're ready to cook, mix together the crispy coating ingredients in a small bowl. Remove the chicken strips from the buttermilk and coat them in the flour mix.

3 Heat the oil in your deep fat fryer to 180°C – you will need about 2 litres depending on the size of your fryer. If you don't have a deep fat fryer, you'll need a thermometer or temperature probe, a deep saucepan and about a litre of vegetable oil – your pot should be no more than one third full.

4 Deep fry the chicken pieces in the oil for 3-5 minutes or until golden brown and cooked through. Remove to a baking sheet lined with kitchen paper.

5 To make the sauce, place the gochujang, honey, sugar, soy sauce, garlic, ginger and sesame oil in a saucepan and stir together. Bring to the boil, then simmer for 5 minutes until thickened. Add the chicken pieces and carefully toss together until the chicken is coated in the sauce. Serve topped with the spring onions and sesame seeds.

CHEF'S NOTE: You can find gochujang paste in any Asian supermarket or specialist grocery shop.

A Bit
Posh

Sometimes you want to get a little bit fancy in the kitchen. Whether you're looking to impress a date, celebrate a big occasion with family, or just treat yourself, it's great to be able to whip up something posh. As a chef, I'm used to making fine-dining food, but you don't need consommé, foam or a red wine reduction to make a really special dish. Knowing how to prepare proper carbonara, perfect steak or pan-fried scallops is all you need to take things to the next level.

Prawn and Pesto Tagliatelle

If you're not a big fan of prawns, you can leave them out or swap them for chicken breast. This is a really easy dish to customize, so get creative and make it your own.

Serves 4

— 400g tagliatelle

For the pesto
— 1 teaspoon sea salt
— 2 cloves of garlic, peeled
— 25g pine nuts, toasted in a dry frying pan
— 1 bunch of fresh basil
— 40g Parmesan cheese, grated
— 100ml extra virgin olive oil

For the prawns
— 250g fresh prawns
— 1 teaspoon olive oil
— a pinch of sea salt
— 250ml of white wine
— juice of ½ lemon
— 1 fresh red chilli, deseeded and finely sliced
— freshly ground black pepper

To serve
— freshly grated Parmesan cheese
— fresh basil leaves

1 Cook the pasta in salted boiling water according to the packet instructions.
2 To make the pesto, grind the salt and garlic in a mortar and pestle until a paste forms. Add in the toasted pine nuts, basil, Parmesan and olive oil and pound everything together until you have a smooth sauce.
3 Cook the prawns in a large hot pan over a high heat for about 2 minutes with the oil and salt, then add the white wine, lemon juice and sliced chilli. Reduce the liquid by half, then add in the pesto and cook for another 2 minutes. Add in your pasta and some black pepper and toss.
4 Serve with grated Parmesan cheese and fresh basil leaves scattered over.

Proper Carbonara with Lemon and Thyme Chicken

You can't beat a proper pasta carbonara. Simple but satisfying, it's a classic for a reason. The chicken and thyme make this that bit fancier, perfect for a special night in. Don't worry about using raw eggs – they cook off in the hot pasta to make a delicious silky sauce.

Serves 2

— 200g tagliatelle
— 3 egg yolks, beaten with 1 whole egg
— 50g Parmesan cheese, grated
— 2 chicken breasts, skin on
— salt and freshly ground black pepper
— olive oil
— 1 teaspoon butter
— juice of 1 lemon
— a few sprigs of thyme, leaves picked and chopped
— 80g smoked bacon, diced

To serve
— zest of 1 lemon
— 2 teaspoons flat-leaf parsley, chopped
— freshly grated Parmesan

1 Preheat the oven to 170°C.

2 Cook the pasta in salted boiling water according to the instructions on the packet, then drain using a colander, reserving a cupful of the cooking water for later. Whisk the eggs with the grated Parmesan in a jug.

3 While your pasta is cooking you can get on with the chicken. Season the chicken breasts generously with salt and pepper. Heat a drizzle of olive oil in a frying pan on a medium heat and add the chicken breasts, skin side down. After about 5 minutes the chicken should be lightly golden; flip them over and add the butter, lemon juice and thyme to the pan. Once the butter starts to foam, start basting the chicken, lifting the juices from the pan with a spoon and drizzling it over the meat, for 2 minutes. This gives you unbelievably juicy chicken. Transfer the chicken to a baking sheet and finish off in the preheated oven for about 8 minutes, until cooked through.

4 Give the pan a quick wipe down with kitchen paper, then fry the bacon on a high heat until all the fat is rendered out and the bacon crisps up. Take the pan off the heat and give it a couple of minutes to cool down – if the pan is too hot, you'll end up with scrambled eggs! Transfer the cooked pasta into the pan with the cup of pasta water and the egg mixture. Stir everything together quickly until it all starts to emulsify and you can see the delicious sauce coming together.

5 Remove the chicken from the oven and slice thinly, then place over the pasta and top with fresh lemon zest, parsley and Parmesan to taste.

Garlic Butter

Have you ever made your own butter? It's a doddle to make, tastes great and it'll really impress your friends at your next swanky dinner party. You can use this garlic butter in loads of ways – on steak, pasta or slathered on a baguette and baked for the best garlic bread you've ever had.

— 500ml double cream
— 1 teaspoon salt
— 4 cloves of garlic, minced
— 1 teaspoon finely chopped fresh parsley

1 Whisk the cream in a stand mixer on a high speed until the butter splits from the cream. This should take about 6 minutes. You should be left with buttermilk too; you can keep this to use in other recipes, like the Irish Guinness bread, if you like.

2 Wash the resulting butter in cold water until the water runs clear.

3 In a bowl, combine the butter, salt, minced garlic and parsley. I find it easiest to do this in a stand mixer with the paddle attachment, but you can use a wooden spoon and do it by hand too.

4 Wrap the garlic butter in cling film and refrigerate for 1 hour. Slice to use as needed.

CHEF'S NOTE: Store the wrapped butter in the fridge for up to one week, or wrap in a double layer of foil and freeze for up to one month.

Irish Guinness Bread

This is hands down the nicest bread I have ever tasted – and, in my opinion, just a little bit posher than regular soda bread.

Makes 2 loaves

— 550g wholemeal flour
— 140g plain flour
— 2 teaspoons baking soda
— 1 teaspoon salt
— 1 tablespoon brown sugar
— 60g rolled oats, plus extra for sprinkling
— 30g unsalted butter, softened at room temperature
— 450ml buttermilk
— 200ml Guinness
— 250g black treacle

1 Preheat the oven to 170°C and grease two 450g loaf tins.

2 Sieve the flours, baking soda and salt together into a large bowl and whisk to combine, then stir through the brown sugar.

3 Add in the oats and the soft butter and mix with a wooden spoon until fully combined. Add in the buttermilk, Guinness and treacle slowly, mixing as you go. Divide between the two greased bread tins and lightly score the top of the dough once with the tip of a sharp knife. Sprinkle the tops with oats and bake in the preheated oven for 40–45 minutes. Test to see they are done by sticking a knife in – if it comes out clean, they are ready.

CHEF'S NOTE: This is great toasted and topped with loads of butter and jam, but my favourite way to have it is dipped in the potato and leek soup on page 48 – a match made in heaven.

Smoked Bacon and Chorizo Bolognese

When I was little my nana often made me spag bol and it's still one of my favourite dinners, but adding chorizo and bacon really takes it to the next level. Using the slow cooker means this is a super-low-stress way to serve something fancy at a dinner party, but if you don't have a slow cooker you can make it on the hob.

Serves 4

— 250g beef mince
— 100g chorizo, chopped
— 100g smoked bacon, chopped
— 1 onion, finely diced
— 1 carrot, peeled and finely diced
— 1 stalk of celery, finely diced
— 2 cloves of garlic, minced
— 100ml red wine
— 250ml beef stock
— 25g tomato paste
— 200g chopped tomatoes (½ a tin)
— 100ml tomato passata
— 200ml milk
— salt and freshly ground black pepper
— leaves from 1 sprig of fresh thyme
— 400g spaghetti

To serve
— a handful of fresh parsley, chopped
— freshly grated Parmesan cheese

1 Brown off the beef, chorizo and smoked bacon in a large saucepan.

2 Add in the chopped vegetables, garlic and thyme, and sweat until softened. Add in the red wine and reduce by half, then add the beef stock, bring it back to a simmer and add the tomato paste, chopped tomatoes, passata and milk (trust me on the milk, it really works!). Season with salt and pepper.

3 Transfer your meat sauce to a slow cooker and cook on a low heat for 5 hours.

4 Cook the pasta in boiling salted water following the packet instructions. Divide the pasta between four plates, top with the sauce and serve with fresh parsley and Parmesan cheese.

Slow-cooked Meatball Marinara

This is my take on the Subway classic. These meatballs freeze well, so make a double batch and stick the leftovers in the freezer as a treat for your future self.

Serves 4

— 300g beef mince
— 1 large onion, diced
— 40g breadcrumbs
— leaves from 1 sprig of fresh thyme
— salt and freshly ground black pepper
— 2 eggs, beaten
— olive oil, for frying

For the sauce
— 150g smoked bacon lardons
— 1 fresh red chilli, deseeded and diced
— 500g tomato passata
— 200g plum tomatoes (½ a tin)
— 1 tablespoon paprika
— 1 tablespoon garlic powder
— leaves from 1 sprig of fresh thyme

To serve
— 4 baguettes or soft rolls
— grated mozzarella cheese
— handful flat-leaf parsley leaves, finely chopped
— Emotional sauce (see page 190)

1 Start by making your meatballs. Mix the beef mince, onion, breadcrumbs, thyme, egg, and salt together and roll into golf ball-sized meatballs. Drizzle a little oil into a frying pan and fry over a medium to high heat until golden brown – they will still be raw in the middle so don't taste them yet! Set aside for now.

2 To make the sauce, put a little more oil into the same pan and sweat off the bacon and chilli before adding all the remaining ingredients. Scrape the bottom of the pan with a wooden spoon to get all the meaty bits into the sauce, then crush everything down and let the sauce simmer for 10 minutes.

3 Put the meatballs into a slow cooker, pour this sauce over them and cook on low for 5 hours.

4 To serve, split and toast your baguettes or rolls under a grill, then fill with the meatballs, plenty of grated mozzarella cheese, a sprinkling of chopped fresh parsley and a dollop of emotional sauce.

CHEF'S NOTE: These are also great served over pasta or on a fresh ciabatta roll smothered in garlic butter.

Pan-fried Chicken Alfredo Pasta

I love this dish with all my heart, even if I struggle to walk after a plateful of it. Saving some of your pasta water to add in at the end is the key to getting that amazingly smooth, rich cheese sauce.

Serves 2

- 2 chicken breasts
- salt and freshly ground black pepper
- 2 teaspoons olive oil
- 200g spaghetti
- 300ml chicken stock
- 2 cloves of garlic, minced
- 350ml cream
- 100g Parmesan cheese, grated
- 1 teaspoon freshly ground nutmeg

To serve
- freshly grated Parmesan cheese
- a handful of fresh flat-leaf parsley, chopped

1 Preheat the oven to 180°C. Line a baking sheet with baking paper.

2 Season the chicken breasts with salt and pepper, then pan fry them in the oil on a high heat until golden brown. Transfer them to the baking sheet and finish cooking them in the preheated oven for 10–12 minutes.

3 Cook the spaghetti in salted boiling water according to the instructions on the packet. Drain in a colander, reserving a cup of the pasta water for later.

4 Put the chicken stock, garlic and cream into a large saucepan over a medium-low heat and let this reduce by half before stirring in the Parmesan and nutmeg. Season with salt and pepper.

5 Add the pasta and pasta water to the sauce in the pan and toss to combine. Slice the chicken breasts and arrange on top of the pasta, garnish with more Parmesan and some chopped fresh parsley and enjoy!

Katsu Curry Salmon with Stir-fried Noodles

This is a cracker of a dish, full of spicy goodness. It's perfect for when you have friends round for dinner and want to make something a little bit different.

Serves 4

For the katsu curry sauce
— 100g butter
— 1 teaspoon vegetable oil
— 1 red pepper, chopped
— 1 green pepper, chopped
— 1 yellow pepper, chopped
— 4 cloves of garlic, minced
— 1 teaspoon ground cumin
— 1 teaspoon garam masala
— 1 teaspoon ground turmeric
— 1 teaspoon ground coriander
— 1 teaspoon paprika
— a bunch of fresh coriander, chopped
— 200g chopped tomatoes (½ a tin)
— 200ml coconut milk (½ a tin)
— 100g mango chutney

For the salmon
— 4 salmon fillets
— 2 teaspoons vegetable oil
— a knob of butter

For the noodles
— 400g noodles
— 1 tablespoon sesame oil
— 4 spring onions, sliced

1 To make the sauce, heat the butter and oil over a medium heat in a large saucepan. Add the peppers, garlic and all the spices and fry until the spices are fragrant and the vegetables are beginning to soften. Add in the rest of the sauce ingredients and stir well. Simmer the sauce on a low heat for 8-10 minutes. Blitz with a stick blender until smooth, then set aside.
2 Dry the salmon skin with a paper towel and heat the oil in a frying pan over a high heat. Place the fillets skin side down in the pan and fry for 5 minutes, until crispy. Flip the salmon over and fry for another 3-4 minutes, then add the butter and baste until cooked through.
3 Cook the noodles in salted boiling water for the time given on the packet. Heat the sesame oil in a wok and add the spring onion. Fry for a few minutes, then toss in the drained noodles so they get coated in the oil.
4 Serve each salmon fillet on a bed of stir-fried noodles, pouring the katsu sauce over.

Pan-fried Scallops with Champagne Sauce, Mussels and Basil Oil

There's no better way to get fancy in the kitchen than with some seared scallops. Fresh scallops can be hard to find, but lots of supermarkets have them frozen now and they're well worth hunting down for a special occasion dinner.

Serves 4

— 12 scallops, roes removed
— 2 teaspoons vegetable oil
— a generous knob of butter
— 200g mussels
— 150ml Champagne
— 2 cloves of garlic, minced

For the sauce
— 1 shallot, finely chopped
— 1 teaspoon vegetable oil
— 100ml Champagne
— 100ml white wine vinegar
— 300ml cream
— 150g cold butter, diced
— squeeze of lemon juice
— salt and freshly-ground black pepper

To serve
— rocket or watercress (optional)
— 2 tablespoons basil oil (page 201)

1 Sear the scallops for 1 minute on a high heat in the vegetable oil, then flip them over and add the butter. Baste the scallops in the melted butter for 2 minutes, until they are cooked through.

2 Cook the mussels in a big pot on a high heat with the Champagne and the garlic until the shells open up. This should take about 3-4 minutes. Drain the mussels and leave to one side for now.

3 For the sauce, fry the shallot in 1 teaspoon vegetable oil, add in the Champagne and the white wine vinegar and reduce until almost all the liquid has evaporated – you'll be left with a sticky shallot syrup. Reduce the heat to low and add in the cream. Reduce this by half and take the pan off the heat. Immediately whisk in the butter one cube at a time until a thick sauce is achieved. Finally, add the lemon juice and salt and pepper to taste.

4 To serve, spread a generous spoonful of the Champagne sauce on the plate and top with three scallops and some mussels. Finish with a handful of rocket or watercress, if you like, and a drizzle of basil oil.

CHEF'S NOTE: If you want to turn this into even more of a feast, serve alongside a big pile of perfect mashed potatoes (see page 8).

Homemade Pasta

Making pasta from scratch might seem like a lot of effort, but try it and you'll see it's not difficult at all once you've had a bit of practice. It tastes a million times better than shop-bought pasta and I actually find making my own pasta really relaxing!

Serves 4

— 250g Tipo 00 flour (a bread and pasta flour available in specialty shops)
— 1 egg (corn-fed, free-range eggs are best)
— 3 egg yolks (corn-fed, free-range eggs are best)
— ½ teaspoon salt
— 1 teaspoon olive oil
— 1 teaspoon water
— flour or semolina, for dusting if making by hand

1 Put the flour in a mound on a countertop or other clean flat surface and create a well in the middle. Pour the egg, egg yolks, salt, olive oil and water into the well. Using a fork, whisk all the wet ingredients together in the well and gradually incorporate the flour from the edges. Slowly add more flour and after a while a paste will begin to form.

2 Continue to work more flour into the paste and a soft dough will form; at this point switch to using your hands. As soon as the dough is kneadable and no longer sticky, stop adding flour – you likely won't need all of it. If your dough feels too dry at this stage, you can add an extra drop of olive oil. Knead the dough until no flour is visible and it's very smooth. This will take at least ten minutes.

3 Wrap your dough in cling film and rest in the fridge for 30 minutes.

4 Cut the dough in half and roll it out so it fits through the lasagne attachment of your pasta machine. Adjust the settings on your machine to get the pasta to your desired thickness – I recommend 2mm for tagliatelle. Finally, pass the dough through your tagliatelle attachment. Repeat with the other half of the dough.

5 If you don't have a pasta machine, it's possible to make it entirely by hand but it's a bit of an upper body workout! Cut the dough in half and generously sprinkle your work surface with flour or semolina. Use a floured rolling pin to roll the dough out to a thickness of about 2mm. This will take time, but be patient and you will get there! Then use a sharp knife to slice the dough into long, thin ribbons and you'll have handmade tagliatelle. >

6 Lightly dust the pasta with flour and hang it up in your kitchen for 30 minutes, until stiff – I use clothes hangers for this! This will ensure that the flour has absorbed all the egg and cooks properly later on.

7 To cook the pasta, bring a large pot of water to the boil, add plenty of salt and add in your desired amount of pasta. Boil for 3-5 minutes, stirring every so often to stop the pasta from sticking together. Drain and serve with your favourite sauce, or try making the carbonara on page 111 or the pasta aglio e olio on page 128.

Pasta Aglio e Olio

The name of this sexy pasta dish from Naples simply means 'pasta with garlic and oil', and it really is that simple to make. I came across this dish on TikTok one day and it just looked so fun and seductive. Give it a go – you know you want to.

Serves 2

- 200g linguine or tagliatelle
- 200ml olive oil
- 3 cloves of garlic, finely sliced
- 2 teaspoons chilli flakes, plus extra to serve

To serve
- a handful of fresh flat-leaf parsley, finely chopped
- freshly ground black pepper
- Parmesan cheese (optional)

1 Cook the pasta in salted boiling water according to the instructions on the packet.
2 Heat the olive oil in a large pan, add the garlic and cook on a low to mediumeat just until it starts to turn golden – be careful not to burn it! Scatter in the chilli flakes and mix through.
3 By now your pasta will be cooked. Drain it in a colander, reserving a cupful of pasta water, then add it into the oil and chilli mix in the pan with the water, stirring to coat every strand.
4 Serve sprinkled with parsley, black pepper and a few extra chilli flakes. Grate some Parmesan over as well if you fancy it.

The Perfect Steak

Here it is: every good chef's pride and joy, the main event, a thing of absolute beauty – the perfect steak. In this recipe, I'll teach you how to master the art of cooking steaks the right way.

Serves 1

— 1 sirloin, rib-eye or t-bone steak, about 350g
— salt and freshly ground black pepper
— vegetable oil
— a few sprigs of fresh thyme
— 2 cloves of garlic, chopped
— 1 tablespoon butter

To serve
— Dijon mustard
— triple-cooked chips (page 15)

1 Take the steak out of the fridge 30 minutes before you want to cook it to allow it to come up to room temperature.

2 Preheat the oven to 170°C.

3 Season the steaks well with salt and pepper. Drizzle a small amount of vegetable oil into a frying pan on a high heat. When the oil starts to smoke, add the steak and sear on high heat for 2 minutes on one side. Using a tongs or other long-handled implement, sear the side sides of the steak for about 30 seconds per side. Flip it over and sear the other side for a further 2 minutes, then add in the thyme, garlic and butter.

4 Once the butter starts foaming, baste the steak with it for 1 minute, then remove the steak to an oven-proof plate or dish and put in the preheated oven for 3 minutes. Remove and let the steak rest, tented with tin foil, for 8 minutes.

5 Slice and serve with some Dijon mustard and triple-cooked chips.

CHEF'S NOTE: Don't be shy when you're seasoning your steak. A lot of the salt will be lost in the pan when you're frying, so add a little more seasoning than you think you'll need.

To make this even more lush, use some of the garlic butter on page 112 to baste your steak.

Around the World

Food inspiration is everywhere. Working in restaurant kitchens, I've had the chance to cook alongside chefs from all around the world who've inspired me to bring new and exciting flavours into my own dishes. There's a bit of everything in this chapter, from aloo tikki bites from Bangladesh and chicken Maryland, an American classic, to chicken katsu curry from Japan.

Aloo Tikki Bites

I learned this recipe from a brilliant chef from Bangladesh who I worked alongside in a restaurant kitchen. It's all my favourite spices in a delicious deep-fried potato cake – what's not to like about that?

Makes 10-12 balls

— 500g mashed potato (page 8)
— ½ teaspoon ground cumin
— ½ teaspoon garam masala
— ½ teaspoon ground turmeric
— ½ teaspoon ground coriander
— ½ teaspoon garlic powder
— a handful of fresh coriander, finely chopped
— 50g frozen peas, thawed
— 100g plain flour
— 3 eggs, beaten with a splash of milk
— 200g panko breadcrumbs
— 1–2 litres vegetable oil

To serve
— cucumber raita (page 197)
— mango chutney

1 In a large bowl, mix the mashed potato, spices, coriander and thawed frozen peas together and use your hands to form into golf ball-sized bites. Transfer to a baking sheet lined with baking paper and freeze for 30 minutes.

2 To make the coating, put the flour, eggs and breadcrumbs in three separate shallow bowls. Coat the balls first in the flour, then the eggs and finally the breadcrumbs.

3 Heat the oil in your deep fat fryer to 170°C - you will need about 2 litres depending on the size of your fryer. If you don't have a deep fat fryer, you'll need a thermometer or temperature probe, a deep saucepan and about a litre of vegetable oil - your pot should be no more than one-third full.

4 Deep fry the aloo tikki balls until golden brown, transferring to a plate lined with kitchen paper when they're done. Serve with cucumber raita and your favourite mango chutney.

Crispy Duck and Hoisin Tacos

I don't remember the first time I had duck, but I definitely remember the first time I tasted these tacos! Duck is quite fatty, which makes it super tender and packed full of flavour, so this is definitely worth trying if you find duck breasts in your local supermarket. You don't have to make the tortillas yourself, but it's easier than you'd think!

Serves 2–3

— 2 duck breasts, fat removed, sliced into strips
— 2 tablespoons Japanese soy sauce
— 2 tablespoons rice wine vinegar
— 2 tablespoons hoisin sauce
— 1 tablespoon Chinese five-spice powder
— 100g plain flour
— 3 eggs, beaten with a splash of milk
— 200g panko breadcrumbs
— 1–2 litres vegetable oil

For the flour tortillas
— 250g plain flour
— 1 tablespoon baking powder
— 1/4 teaspoon salt
— 125g water
— 3 tablespoons olive oil

To serve
— Japanese mayo (page 180)
— spring onions, julienned
— cucumber, julienned
— hoisin sauce

1 Put the duck strips in a bowl with the soy sauce, rice wine vinegar, hoisin sauce and five-spice powder. Marinate for at least 1 hour, covered, in the fridge.

2 Make the flour tortillas by mixing all the dry ingredients in a bowl, then add the water and olive oil and mix well until a dough forms. Divide the dough into six evenly-sized balls. Roll each ball out into a 12cm round tortilla. Fry the tortillas in a hot, dry frying pan for 1 minute on each side. Keep warm while you get the duck ready.

3 Put the flour, eggs and panko breadcrumbs in three separate shallow bowls. Coat the duck first in the flour, then the eggs and finally the panko breadcrumbs.

4 Heat the oil in your deep fat fryer to 180°C - you will need about 2 litres depending on the size of your fryer. If you don't have a deep fat fryer, you'll need a thermometer or temperature probe, a deep saucepan and about a litre of vegetable oil - your pot should be no more than one-third full.

5 Deep fry the duck strips for 8 minutes, until crispy, and golden brown and cooked through, transferring to a plate lined with kitchen paper when they're done.

6 Spread a little Japanese mayo on each tortilla. Top with the crispy duck, spring onions and cucumber and drizzle with a little extra hoisin.

Salt and Chilli Chicken Tray

The inspiration for this comes from closer to home – my favourite Chinese takeaway. This is a Friday night classic for a reason. If you're making this for someone who is gluten intolerant, you can use gluten-free flour, it works just as well.

Serves 4

— 100g plain flour
— ½ teaspoon garlic powder
— ½ teaspoon paprika
— ½ teaspoon Chinese 5-spice powder
— 3 eggs, beaten with a splash of milk
— 4 chicken breasts, sliced thinly
— 1–2 litres vegetable oil
— 4 cloves of garlic, minced
— 2 red bell peppers, deseeded and roughly chopped
— 2 green bell peppers, deseeded and roughly chopped
— 2 fresh red chillies, deseeded and sliced
— 1 generous tablespoon honey

To serve
— thinly sliced spring onions
— chilli flakes
— sea salt

1 Mix the flour in a bowl with the spices. Put the beaten eggs in another bowl. Dip the chicken pieces first in the flour, then in the eggs, then back in the flour again, transferring them to a plate when done.

2 Heat the oil in your deep fat fryer to 170°C - you will need about 2 litres depending on the size of your fryer. If you don't have a deep fat fryer, you'll need a thermometer or temperature probe, a deep saucepan and about a litre of vegetable oil - your pot should be no more than one-third full.

3 Deep fry the chicken pieces until crispy and cooked through, transferring to a plate lined with kitchen paper when they're done.

4 Heat a tablespoon of vegetable oil in a large frying pan or wok over a medium to high heat, then add in the garlic, peppers, chillies and honey. Cook until everything is nice and sticky. Add the crispy chicken pieces to the vegetable mix. Toss everything together to coat the chicken in the honey. Serve sprinkled with sliced spring onions, chilli flakes and sea salt.

Chicken Katsu Curry

This popular Japanese dish combines a fried, breaded chicken breast with a mild and creamy curry sauce. It's the perfect curry for anyone who doesn't like it too spicy, and served with rice or chips this dish is a winner all round.

Serves 4

For the chicken
— 4 chicken breasts
— 500ml buttermilk
— 100g plain flour
— 3 eggs, beaten with a splash of milk
— 100g fresh or panko breadcrumbs

For the katsu curry sauce
— 100g butter
— 1 teaspoon vegetable oil
— 1 red pepper, deseeded and chopped
— 1 green pepper, deseeded and chopped
— 1 yellow pepper, deseeded and chopped
— 4 cloves of garlic, minced
— 1 teaspoon ground cumin
— 1 teaspoon garam masala
— 1 teaspoon ground turmeric
— 1 teaspoon ground coriander
— 1 teaspoon paprika
— a bunch of fresh coriander, chopped
— 200g chopped tomatoes (½ a tin)
— 200ml coconut milk (½ a tin)
— 100g mango chutney

To serve
— triple-cooked chips (page 15) or cooked short-grain rice
— a handful of fresh coriander, chopped (optional)
— spring onions, sliced (optional)

1 Put the chicken breasts into a bowl, pour over the buttermilk and marinate in the fridge for at least 1 hour or up to 24 hours – the longer you marinate, the more tender the chicken will be.
2 Preheat the oven to 180°C and line a baking sheet with baking paper.
3 Put the flour, beaten eggs and breadcrumbs in three separate bowls. Dip the chicken in the flour, eggs, then the breadcrumbs. Arrange on the baking sheet and bake in your preheated oven for 12–15 minutes, until golden and crispy and cooked through.
4 To make the sauce, heat the butter and oil over a medium heat in a large saucepan. Add the peppers, garlic and all the spices and fry until the spices are fragrant and the vegetables are beginning to soften. Add in the rest of the ingredients and stir well. Simmer the sauce on a low heat for 15-20 minutes. Blitz with a stick blender until smooth.
5 To serve, slice the chicken into strips, place on top of chips or rice and pour over the katsu sauce. Scatter with some chopped fresh coriander or sliced spring onions, if you like.

CHEF'S NOTE: If your curry sauce is too thick after you blend it, you can add a splash of water or a little more coconut milk to get your desired consistency.

Crispy Tofu Uramaki Rolls

I'm not saying this is real, authentic sushi, but everyone who's tried it agrees that it tastes unreal. Most supermarkets sell sushi sheets and sushi rice, so it's not hard to get your hands the ingredients. It takes a while to get the hang of this, but it's fun to make – especially if you invite your mates round and turn it into a sushi party.

Serves 6-8

For the rice
— 80ml rice wine vinegar
— 2 tablespoons sugar
— 300g sushi rice

For the crispy tofu
— 200g tofu
— 50ml dark soy sauce
— 100ml rice wine vinegar
— 1/4 teaspoon freshly ground black pepper
— 100g plain flour
— 3 eggs, beaten
— 200g panko breadcrumbs
— 125ml vegetable oil

To assemble
— 1 packet of seaweed sushi sheets
— Japanese mayo (page 180), plus extra for dipping
— 1 cucumber, halved lengthways, deseeded and cut into thin strips
— 1 avocado, sliced (optional)
— 3 tablespoons sesame seeds, toasted

1 Put the rice wine vinegar and sugar in a pot over a low heat. Cook, stirring occasionally, until all the sugar has dissolved. Remove from the heat and allow to cool.
2 In a bowl, cover the rice with cold water and gently stir until the water becomes cloudy – this means the rice is releasing starch. Repeat this process three times, draining the rice each time in a colander. The water should be running clear by the third time.
3 Put the washed rice in a large pot and pour over enough cold water to come about 5cm above the rice. Once the rice comes to a boil, turn the heat down to a low simmer and cook until all the water has evaporated, about 10 minutes. Keep an eye on your rice to make sure it doesn't begin to burn. Remove from the heat, put on a lid and allow to sit for 10 minutes, then spread the rice out on a tray.
4 Sprinkle the vinegar syrup over the rice while it's still warm and use a fork to separate the grains so there are no large clumps. Allow to cool on the tray until it reaches room temperature.
5 Cut the tofu into thin rectangular strips, transfer to a bowl and marinate in the soy sauce, rice vinegar and salt and pepper for 10 minutes. Put the flour, eggs and panko into three separate shallow bowls and coat the tofu strips first in flour, then egg, and finally panko.

6 Heat the vegetable oil in a large pan, then shallow fry the coated tofu strips on a medium to high heat until golden brown all over. Remove to a plate lined with kitchen paper.

7 To make your sushi, place a sushi mat or clean tea towel on a flat surface and cover with a large piece of cling film. Place a seaweed sheet on the cling film and spread sushi rice evenly on top of it. Your rice should be nice and sticky in texture.

8 Flip the seaweed sheet over and spread a thin layer of Japanese mayo on the seaweed 2.5cm from the end closest to you (see the photos). Top this with a layer of cucumber, tofu strips and avocado (if using). Using your mat or tea towel and cling film, begin to roll your sushi from the end closest to you, applying gentle pressure to squeeze out any air and tucking the seaweed in as you go.

9 Peel off the cling film and cut the roll into eight even slices using a very sharp knife. Sprinkle over the sesame seeds and serve with extra Japanese mayo for dipping.

CHEF'S NOTE: Once you've made your sushi rice it will be safe at room temperature for up to 6 hours, so you can start prepping this a couple of hours in advance if you need to. If you have any rice left over, it pairs perfectly with the chicken katsu curry on page 142.

To make this vegan, swap the mayo in the Japanese Mayo for a vegan alternative.

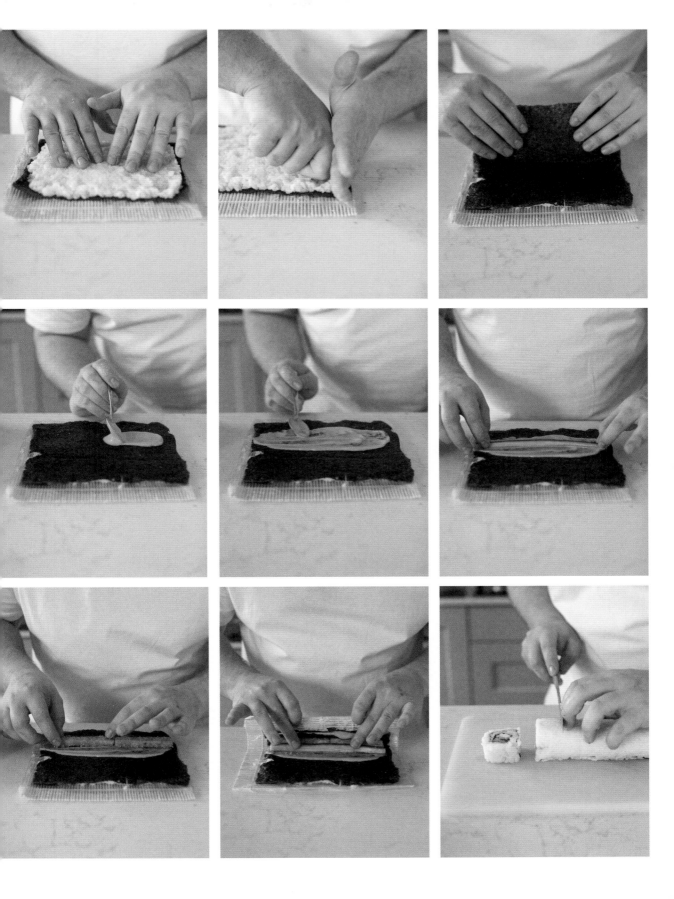

Curried Fishcakes with Lime Mayo

Fishcakes are the ideal party food and a great way to use up leftover mash. Adding curry powder and chilli gives these a little something extra and they're perfect paired with the zesty lime mayo.

Makes 10-12 fishcakes

— 300g mixed fish (smoked haddock, salmon, cod), cut into small dice
— 250g mashed potato (page 8)
— 1 red chilli, finely sliced
— 1 tablespoon finely chopped fresh coriander
— 1 tablespoon finely chopped fresh dill
— 1 tablespoon finely chopped fresh chives
— 2 teaspoons medium curry powder
— a generoush pinch of salt
— ¼ teaspoon ground white pepper
— 100g plain flour
— 2 eggs, beaten with a splash of milk
— 150g panko breadcrumbs
— 2 tablespoons olive oil

For the lime mayo
— 4 tablespoons mayonnaise
— 1 teaspoon finely chopped fresh chives
— zest and juice of 1 lime
— freshly ground black pepper

1 Start by mixing the diced fish and mashed potato together in a large bowl with the chilli, herbs, curry powder, salt and white pepper. Mix everything together with a wooden spoon until combined.

2 Shape the potato mixture into small patties – you should get between 10 and 12, depending on how big you make them. Place the fishcakes on a baking sheet lined with baking paper and freeze them for 1 hour until firm.

3 Put the flour, beaten eggs and panko breadcrumbs into three separate shallow bowls. Coat the fishcakes in the flour, then the eggs, and finally the breadcrumbs and return to the baking sheet for now.

4 To fry the fishcakes, heat the olive oil in a frying pan over a medium heat. Shallow fry the fishcakes until golden brown all over and cooked through, 5-6 minutes on each side.

5 For the lime mayo, mix the mayonnaise with the chives, lime zest and juice, and a generous grinding of black pepper. Serve the fishcakes with the mayo for dipping.

Chicken Maryland

Chicken, banana and bacon might sound like another one of my mad experiments, but believe it or not this dish has been around since the 19th century – proof that mental flavour mash-ups aren't a new invention! Don't knock this until you try it – banana and bacon are absolutely lush together.

Serves 4

- 4 chicken breasts, butterflied
- 500ml buttermilk
- ¼ teaspoon ground black pepper
- 100g plain flour
- 3 eggs, beaten with ¼ teaspoon salt
- 100g fresh breadcrumbs, mixed with ¼ teaspoon black pepper
- 300ml vegetable oil

For the bacon and banana bites
- 10 smoked streaky bacon rashers
- 2 bananas, peeled and cut into 4cm-long chunks, to give about 10 pieces
- 2 tablespoons maple syrup

For the sauce
- 1 tablespoon vegetable oil
- 1 shallot, finely chopped
- 1 fresh red chilli, finely chopped
- 1 red pepper, chopped
- 300ml chicken stock
- 200ml fresh cream
- 50g tinned sweetcorn, drained
- salt
- snipped fresh chives, to garnish

1 To butterfly the chicken breasts, cut each one vertically through the middle, stopping before they are completely cut in half. Spread them out on a board so they are flat, and that's it! Put the butterflied chicken breasts in a large bowl with the buttermilk and black pepper and leave to marinate for at least an hour or up to 24 hours in the fridge.

2 When you're ready to cook, preheat your oven to 170°C.

3 Start by making your bacon and banana bites. Wrap one slice of streaky bacon around each banana chunk and brush them with the maple syrup. Transfer to a baking sheet lined with baking paper and cook in the preheated oven for 10–15 minutes.

4 Put the flour, eggs and breadcrumbs in three separate shallow bowls. Coat the butterflied chicken breasts in the flour, then the eggs, then the breadcrumbs. Heat the vegetable oil in a frying pan on a medium to high heat until it reaches 170°C. Shallow fry the chicken until it's golden and crispy, about 2 minutes on each side.

5 To make the sauce, heat the oil in a large frying pan over a medium heat. Add in the shallot, chilli and red pepper and fry for 3 minutes, until they begin to soften. Pour in the chicken stock and cream, turn the heat down to low and reduce until it's thick enough to coat the back of a spoon. Add the sweetcorn and season with salt to taste.

6 To serve, pour some of the sauce on each plate, top with a chicken breast and a couple of bacon banana bites. Garnish with fresh chives.

CHEF'S NOTE: Butterflying the chicken breasts makes sure they cook quickly on the pan, giving you juicy meat and a gorgeous golden crumb.

Chicken Tikka Masala with Spiced Rice

You might think this is an Indian classic, but it was actually invented in Britain in the 1970s by a Bangladeshi chef! It's full of all the Indian flavours we love, though, and it's ideal on a chilly night with an ice-cold beverage.

Serves 4

— 4 large chicken breasts, chopped

For the marinade
— 150g coconut yoghurt
— 2 teaspoons ground coriander
— 2 teaspoons paprika
— 2 teaspoons garam masala
— 1 teaspoon chilli powder
— 2 fresh red chillies, deseeded and finely chopped
— a thumb-sized piece of fresh ginger, peeled and minced
— 3 cloves of garlic, minced
— juice of 1 lemon

For the sauce
— 2 teaspoons vegetable oil
— 2 large onions, sliced
— 2 teaspoons ground coriander
— 2 teaspoons paprika
— 2 teaspoons garam masala
— 1 teaspoon chilli powder
— salt and freshly ground black pepper
— 500ml tomato passata
— 2 tablespoons tomato paste
— 1 teaspoon coconut oil
— a knob of butter
— 150g coconut yoghurt

For the spiced rice
— 1 tablespoon vegetable oil
— 2 teaspoons ground turmeric
— 2 star anise
— 1 cardamom pod
— 2 shallots, finely diced
— 320g basmati rice
— 1 clove of garlic, grated
— 600ml vegetable stock

To serve
— a handful of fresh coriander, roughly chopped
— naan, toasted

1 First get your chicken marinating. Mix the yoghurt in a large bowl with the coriander, paprika, garam masala, chilli powder, half the chopped chilli, half the ginger and garlic, and the lemon juice. Add the chicken pieces, stir to coat and leave to marinate in the fridge for at least one hour or up to 24 hours.

2 For the sauce, heat the oil in a large pan and sweat off the onions, then add in the remaining fresh chilli and ginger that you prepared for the marinade. Sauté for a minute, then stir in all the spices and season with salt and pepper. Cook over a medium heat for about 10 minutes, until the mixture forms a paste, then add in the tomato passata and tomato paste and cook for a further 10 minutes on a low heat. Blitz until smooth in a blender or food processor.

3 Melt the coconut oil and butter in a separate large pan. Remove the chicken pieces from the marinade, add to the pan and lightly sear just until they start to turn golden. Add in your sauce from the blender and the coconut yoghurt. Simmer for 15–20 minutes, until the chicken is cooked through..

4 While the curry is cooking, prepare your rice. Heat the oil in a large pot and fry all the spices and shallots for about 30 seconds on a high heat, then add the rice and garlic. Mix everything together and cook for another 30 seconds, then add the vegetable stock. Bring to the boil, then turn down to a simmer and cook until all the liquid has been absorbed, about 15 minutes.

5 To serve, pile some rice on a plate, top with the curry and sprinkle over some fresh coriander. Serve with toasted naan.

The
Sweetest
Thing

To me, the sweetest thing in life is food in general. Whether it's coffee and cake while you catch up with a friend or a big dinner with the fam, food has the power to bring people together. If you really want to make people smile, though, there's no doubt that a homemade dessert or some fresh-baked goodies will do the job. How about making a batch of emotional chocolate brownies to share with your mates? Or peppermint Aero cheesecake for a special birthday dinner? And if all you really want to do is treat yourself, you can whip up a Kinder Bueno mug cake in two minutes flat, no sharing required... Whatever you do, just don't skip on the sweet stuff.

Popcorn Ice Cream

I bet you didn't know you could make your own ice cream without a fancy ice cream machine. Double cream and sweetened condensed milk gives you the perfect base for homemade ice cream, and it doesn't need to be churned either – just whip it up, stick in the freezer overnight, and enjoy!

Serves 6

— 600ml double cream
— 100g salted popcorn
— 200g sweetened condensed milk
— 125ml caramel sauce

1 Put the cream in a bowl and mix the popcorn through. Leave to soak for at least 3 hours, then blitz in a food processor until smooth. Strain the mixture into a large bowl through a fine sieve, then add in the sweetened condensed milk.

2 Whisk using a stand mixer or hand-held mixer just until soft peaks start to form, then transfer to a loaf tin. Pour the caramel sauce over and use the tip of a knife to swirl it through the ice cream mixture.

3 Cover with cling film, then freeze for 12 hours. Serve with extra caramel sauce and some more popcorn, if you like.

CHEF'S NOTE: If you feel like getting a bit experimental, replace the popcorn with your favourite cereal.

Mint Chocolate Shake

This is my own take on that famous Paddy's Day mint chocolate shake. You can omit the green food colouring if you don't have any.

Serves 4

— 2 pasteurised egg whites
— 1 tablespoon granulated sugar
— 2 drops of green food colouring
— 4 scoops of vanilla ice cream
— 100g white chocolate drops or buttons
— 400ml full-fat milk
— ½ teaspoon mint extract

To serve
— vanilla ice cream
— fresh mint leaves
— 50g mint-flavoured milk chocolate, grated

1 Whisk the egg whites and the sugar together until soft peaks form, then stir in the green food colouring. Set aside for now.

2 Blitz four scoops of vanilla ice cream with the white chocolate drops, milk and mint extract in a blender until smooth.

3 Divide the milkshake between four tall glasses, then top with a dollop of egg whites, a scoop of ice cream, some fresh mint leaves and a sprinkle of grated mint chocolate.

Peppermint Aero Cheesecake

If you need to make a dessert that's easy but impressive, this is the one for you. Everybody goes mad for this when I make it at home. It's perfect for a special occasion or just a weekend treat.

Makes 8-10 slices

— 300ml double cream
— 170g digestive biscuits
— 100g cocoa powder
— 80g melted butter
— 380g cream cheese
— 100g icing sugar
— 1 teaspoon mint extract
— 1 teaspoon green food colouring
— 120g Aero Peppermint chocolate, crushed

For the topping
— whipped cream
— 100g Aero Peppermint Bubbles, roughly chopped

1 Whip the cream until soft peaks form and set aside for later.
2 Blitz the digestives, cocoa powder and butter in a food processor. Press this mixture into the base of a 25cm springform tin with your hands – this is the base for your cheesecake. Refrigerate while you make the filling.
3 Beat the cream cheese, icing sugar, mint extract and green food coloring together in a large bowl, then fold in the whipped cream and stir the crushed Peppermint Aero through.
4 Spread this mix over the digestive biscuit base in your tin and return to the fridge. Leave to set overnight.
5 When you're ready to serve, unclip the side from the tin and remove the cheesecake to a serving plate. Top with more whipped cream and roughly chopped Aero Peppermint Bubbles.

CHEF'S NOTE: I love mint chocolate, but if you're not a fan, you can omit the green food colouring, swap the mint extract for vanilla extract and use regular milk chocolate Aero instead.

Honeycomb and Chocolate Bites

I don't have that much of a sweet tooth, but even I think these snacks are life-changing. They're perfect any time you need a bite-sized pick-me-up.

Makes approximately xx bites

— 200g sugar
— 100g runny honey
— ½ tablespoon glucose syrup
— 100ml water
— 15g bicarbonate of soda
— 200g milk chocolate, roughly chopped
— a generous pinch of flaky sea salt

1 Line a baking sheet with baking paper and have a spatula and whisk set out on the counter. Once you start making your honeycomb you won't be able to leave the pot unattended, so it helps to have everything ready to go.
2 To make the honeycomb, heat the sugar, honey, glucose syrup and water in a pot over a medium heat, stirring continuously with a whisk until the syrup turns a deep golden colour – about 7 minutes. Take the syrup off the heat, stir in the bicarb and continue whisking for about 10 seconds – the liquid will foam and the honeycomb will begin to form. Use a spatula to pour and spread the resulting honeycomb on a baking sheet lined with baking paper and allow to cool completely.
3 Put the chocolate in a heatproof bowl and melt by microwaving on medium power at intervals of 30 seconds.
4 Chop or snap the honeycomb into bite-sized pieces and dip into the melted chocolate. Put the chunks on a baking sheet lined with fresh baking paper and sprinkle with a little flaky sea salt before allowing to set.

Gooey Cookies

There's nothing like the smell of fresh cookies baking in the oven. You can forget about buying cookies ever again after trying these beauties. Try dipping one into hot chocolate for the ultimate chocolate treat.

Makes 8-10

— 160g butter
— 160g brown sugar
— 2 teaspoons vanilla extract
— 1 egg
— 200g plain flour
— 1 teaspoon baking powder
— 105g milk chocolate chips
— 105g white chocolate chips

1 Preheat the oven to 170°C and line a baking sheet with baking paper.
2 Mix the butter and sugar together with a hand-held mixer until nice and fluffy. Add in the vanilla extract and the egg, mix, then fold in the rest of the ingredients with a wooden spoon – don't overwork the mixture or it will ruin the cookies. Mix until a dough forms, then roll golf ball-sized balls of the dough and place on the prepared baking sheet, well spaced out. You should have enough to make between 8 and 10 cookies.
3 Bake in the preheated oven for 8–10 minutes, until firm on the outside but a bit gooey in the middle – they will harden further when they come out of the oven. Leave to cool on the tray for a few minutes, then transfer to a wire rack to cool completely.

CHEF'S NOTE: These are better if you make the dough the day before you want to cook them. Once you've made the dough, form it into a disc, wrap in cling film and put in the fridge overnight. Bring to room temperature before rolling into balls and following the rest of the instructions.

Emotional Chocolate Brownies

It's hard to describe how good these are. They're super chocolatey with that amazing, fudgy texture that the best brownies always have. These are at their best when you let them go cold before slicing, then gently reheat in the microwave.

Makes 12

— 170g butter
— 170g dark chocolate, broken into pieces
— 260g golden caster sugar
— 4 eggs
— 1 teaspoon vanilla extract
— 70g plain flour
— 30g cocoa powder
— 45g white chocolate, chopped
— 45g milk chocolate, chopped

1 Preheat the oven to 170°C and grease and line a 20cm square brownie tin with baking paper.

2 Put the butter and chocolate into a heatproof bowl over a small pot of simmering water until the chocolate melts, stirring occasionally. The bowl should sit above the water, not touching it.

3 In a separate bowl, whisk the sugar and eggs together until fluffy and turning a pale colour, then add in the vanilla. Sieve in the flour and cocoa powder, then add in the melted chocolate and fold it all together.

4 Pour into your prepared tin, smooth over the top, then sprinkle over the chopped chocolate pieces. Transfer to the preheated oven and bake for 25–30 minutes – there should still be a bit of a wobble in the centre when you remove the tin from the oven. Allow to cool for about an hour, until just warm, before slicing.

CHEF'S NOTE: As good as these are on their own, topping them with a scoop of the popcorn ice cream on page 156 and a generous drizzle of caramel sauce really takes them to the next level.

Kinder Bueno Mug Cake

If you're craving cake but you're too lazy to get baking, a mug cake is the answer. They're perfect for satisfying your sweet tooth and they only take two minutes to whip up. I've made this one with Kinder Bueno because I love it, but you could use any chocolate bar you like.

Makes 1

— butter, for greasing
— 4 tablespoons oats, blitzed in a food processer to make a fine powder
— ½ teaspoon baking powder
— 1 tablespoon cocoa powder
— 4 tablespoons milk
— 1 egg, beaten
— 1 tablespoon Nutella, or your favourite chocolate spread
— 3 squares of Kinder Bueno

1 Grease a large mug with some butter. In a small bowl, mix together the oats, baking powder and cocoa powder. Add the milk and egg and mix until everything is combined.

2 Pour the mixture into your greased mug and top with the Nutella and Kinder Bueno squares. Microwave for 70 seconds on high, keeping an eye on it to make sure your mug doesn't overflow. If the mug cake is still too runny, microwave for 10 seconds at a time until cooked to your liking.

CHEF'S NOTE: To make a gluten free chocolate mug cake, use gluten-free oats and baking powder and any gluten free chocolate spread and chocolate bar.

Edible Cookie Dough

Personally, I think eating the dough is the best part of making cookies, so I came up with this edible cookie dough recipe. It doesn't contain any eggs and heat treating the flour makes it safe to eat raw, so you can dig in.

Serves 8

— 120g plain flour
— 140g light soft brown sugar
— 110g butter, softened
— 1 teaspoon vanilla extract
— a generous pinch of salt
— 2 tablespoons milk
— 150g chocolate chips

1 Start by heat treating your flour – this makes it safe to eat raw. Preheat your oven to 160°C. Spread the flour on a baking sheet with a lip and cover with a sheet of tin foil. Bake in the preheated oven for about 6 minutes, then allow to cool completely.

2 Combine the brown sugar and butter in a large bowl and beat with a hand-held mixer until creamy. Beat in the vanilla extract and salt. Add the flour and mix until a crumbly dough forms, then stir in the milk. Finally, fold in the milk chocolate chips.

Cookie Dough
Ice Cream

Obviously you can just eat your cookie dough with a spoon, but why not take it to the next level and use it to make your own cookie dough ice cream? I think this is even better than Ben & Jerry's!

Serves 6

— 150g edible cookie dough (page 169)
— 200g sweetened condensed milk
— 600ml double cream
— gooey cookies (page 164), to serve

1 Make the edible cookie dough from the recipe on page 169.

2 Pour the sweetened condensed milk and cream into a mixing bowl. Whisk using a stand mixer or hand-held mixer just until soft peaks start to form.

3 Use a teaspoon to scoop small chunks of the cookie dough into the ice cream mix and stir them through. Transfer to a loaf tin, cover with cling film, and freeze for 12 hours. Serve with gooey cookies if you're feeling really indulgent.

Eton Mess

Crunchy meringue, fresh strawberries, strawberry sauce and whipped cream ... yes, please! Simple but tasty, Eton mess is the perfect dessert to have on a hot day. I like to serve mine topped with a scoop of vanilla ice cream, because why not?

Serves 4

— 3 egg whites
— 125g caster sugar, plus 1 teaspoon
— 400g frozen strawberries
— 500ml double cream
— 1 vanilla pod, split lengthways and seeds scraped out

To serve
— 8 fresh strawberries, chopped
— vanilla ice cream
— fresh mint leaves (optional)

1 Preheat the oven to 120°C and line a baking sheet with baking paper.

2 Start by whisking the egg whites in a large mixing bowl until soft peaks form, then add in the 125g of sugar very gradually, whisking between each addition. When the mixture is stiff and glossy, the meringue mix is ready.

3 Dollop large spoonfuls of the meringue onto your prepared baking sheet and cook in the preheated oven for 1 hour. Allow the meringues to cool completely, then roughly crush them with your hands.

4 To make the strawberry sauce, place the strawberries in a saucepan with 1 teaspoon of sugar. Simmer until the strawberries are nice and soft. Allow to cool and blend with a stick blender or in a food processer to form a smooth sauce.

5 Whip the cream until soft peaks form, then fold in the vanilla seeds.

6 To assemble the Eton mess, mix three-quarters of the crushed meringues with the strawberry sauce and chopped strawberries in a bowl. Dollop some cream into four bowls or glasses, followed by some of the strawberry meringue mixture, another layer of cream and another layer of the sauce (reserving some for decoration). Top with scoops of ice cream, drizzle over a little more sauce and scatter the remaining crumbled meringues over the top. Garnish with some fresh mint leaves if you like.

CHEF'S NOTE: When making meringue, it helps to make sure the bowl is completely free from grease or oily residue. Wipe your mixing bowl out with kitchen paper dampened with a drop of lemon juice or white wine vinegar to make sure you get perfect stiff peaks.

Homemade Custard

Custard is one of those things that's way nicer when you make it yourself. Keep a close eye on it when you're cooking and keep stirring so it doesn't stick to the bottom of the pot. This is good hot or cold.

Serves 4-6 as a side

— 550ml milk
— 200ml single cream
— 1 whole vanilla pod, split in half and seeds scraped out
— 5 egg yolks
— 40g caster sugar

1 Heat the milk, cream and the seeds from the vanilla pod together in a saucepan until it's steaming, but don't let it boil. Strain and leave aside to cool slightly.

2 Whisk the egg yolks and sugar together in a bowl until frothy and turning pale, then slowly pour in the slightly warm milk mixture, stirring continuously.

3 Pour this back into the saucepan and very slowly increase the heat from low to medium, stirring the whole time with a rubber spatula, until the mixture is thick enough to coat the back of the spatula. This should take about 8-10 minutes, but be patient and don't be tempted to turn the heat up! Slow and steady is the way to go.

CHEF'S NOTE: If you see lumps of custard sticking to your spatula, take the pot off the heat, place it on a cold heatproof surface and whisk the custard as hard as you can to make it smooth again. Let it cool down a little bit before putting it back on the heat and continuing to cook until it's thickened.

Deep-fried Mars Bars

If you've ever been to Scotland, you know what this one is all about. One of the nicest things ever to come out of my deep fat fryer.

Makes 4

— 1 egg
— 200g plain flour
— 400ml water
— 1–2 litres vegetable oil
— 4 Mars Bars

1 Mix the first three ingredients together in a bowl to form a batter. Line a plate with kitchen paper.

2 Heat the oil in your deep fat fryer to 180°C - you will need about 2 litres depending on the size of your fryer. If you don't have a deep fat fryer, you'll need a thermometer or temperature probe, a deep saucepan and about a litre of vegetable oil - your pot should be no more than one-third full.

3 Coat the Mars Bars in the cold batter and deep fry for 2 minutes. Transfer to the lined plate and allow to cool slightly before serving.

Super Fruit Smoothie

There's nothing nicer on a hot summer day than a fruit smoothie – except for maybe a fruit smoothie topped with a generous scoop of vanilla ice cream. Don't judge me - I'm a chef, not a doctor!

Makes 1

— a handful of frozen mixed berries
— 3 fresh strawberries
— ½ banana, roughly chopped
— 200g natural yoghurt
— 100g coconut milk
— 50g raspberry purée
— 1 or 2 scoops vanilla ice cream

1 Blitz all the ingredients except for 1 tablespoon of the raspberry purée and the ice cream together in a blender until smooth.

2 Pour into a tall glass, drizzle over the remaining raspberry purée, top with the vanilla ice cream and serve with a straw.

CHEF'S NOTE: To turn this into a delicious breakfast smoothie, add 15g rolled oats into the blender with the rest of the ingredients and swap the ice cream for a generous spoonful of Greek yoghurt and a sprinkle of your favourite granola.

A Bit
on the
Side

/

No, I'm not talking about your friend with benefits... I'm talking about dips, dressings, sauces and other cheeky little ways to upgrade your dinner – the good stuff. Personally, I think this is the key chapter. After all, a great sauce can make a dish. Once you've had emotional sauce on a burger, dipped your sushi in Japanese mayo or had a bacon butty smothered in smoked bacon jam, you'll never go back to shop-bought condiments again.

Japanese Mayo

Soy sauce is the ultimate flavour bomb – add all that umami into creamy mayo and you have a sauce that works well with just about anything.

Serves 2-4 as a dip or sauce

— 2 tablespoons good-quality mayonnaise
— 1 tablespoon soy sauce

1 Mix the two ingredients together well until a dark sauce forms. This is amazing with almost any savoury dish!

Garlic Mayo

Have you ever got a takeaway pizza only to realise the delivery driver forgot the garlic dip? Nightmare! If you have a jar of this in the fridge, I guarantee you'll be putting it on everything.

Serves 8 as a dip or sauce

— 250ml olive oil
— 1 whole egg
— 1 teaspoon Dijon mustard
— a pinch of sea salt
— 1 tablespoon white wine vinegar
— 3 cloves of roasted garlic (page 184)
— 2 teaspoons fresh chives, finely chopped

1 Put the olive oil, egg and Dijon mustard in the blender and blitz until just combined. Add the salt, white wine vinegar and roasted garlic and blitz again until you have a smooth sauce. Finally, stir through the finely chopped chives.

2 Put the mayonnaise in a sterilised jar with a lid and store in the fridge for up to five days.

Garlic mayo

Thousand Island dressing

Curried mayo

Emotional sauce

Caesar dressing

Roasted Garlic

You might think you don't need to have a jar of roasted garlic in your fridge, but trust me: you do.

Makes 1 head of roasted garlic

— 1 head of garlic, whole

1 Preheat the oven to 160°C. Wrap the head of garlic in tin foil and place on a baking tray. Bake in the preheated oven for 15 minutes, then allow to cool completely.
2 Unwrap the garlic and slice through the head horizontally so the cloves are exposed. Squeeze the base of the garlic head and the cloves should slide out easily. You can use these in the garlic mayo on page 181, the garlic butter on page 112, or spread on the perfect steak on page 132. This is also unreal just spread on some toast.
3 Put the cloves into a small sterilised jar, pour over enough oil to cover and store in the fridge for up to two weeks.

Sour Cream and Chive Dip

This is the stuff party legends are made of. No matter what the occasion is, at every party, it seems like there's always a bowl of sour cream and chive dip on the table next to a big bowl of crisps. Try this with nachos or spicy wings – lush.

Serves 6-8 as a dip or sauce

— 200g sour cream
— 65g full-fat mayonnaise
— 1 tablespoon finely sliced fresh chives
— juice of ½ lemon
— 1 clove of roasted garlic, mashed with a fork (see the previous page)
— salt and freshly ground black pepper

1 In a bowl, combine the sour cream, mayo, chives, lemon juice and roasted garlic.
2 Stir to combine, then season to taste with salt and freshly ground black pepper.

Caesar Dressing

I made this for the first time when I was making Caesar salad for dinner but forgot to get a bottle of dressing – of course, it tasted way better than the shop-bought stuff. Don't worry if you're not a fan of anchovies, they just add a really nice savoury flavour and don't taste fishy at all.

Serves 8 as a dressing

— 1 egg
— 200ml olive oil
— 4 anchovies, from a tin
— a pinch of sea salt
— 1 teaspoon Dijon mustard
— 1 teaspoon white wine vinegar

1 Blitz all the ingredients together in a blender until smooth.
2 Put the dressing in a sterilised jar with a lid and store in the fridge for up to five days.

CHEF'S NOTE: For the most amazing Caesar salad, throw some roughly chopped baby gem, a handful of the croutons on the next page, some freshly grated Parmesan and cooked smoked bacon lardons into a bowl. Add a squeeze of lemon, some freshly cracked black pepper and ½ a tablespoon of your Caesar dressing. Toss everything together, then drizzle more Caesar dressing over the top.

Sourdough Croutons

Croutons are the easiest way to instantly upgrade any salad, soup or pasta dish and they're the perfect way to use up bread that's gone a bit stale.

Serves 2

— **2 slices of almost-stale sourdough**
— **2 teaspoons olive oil**
— **½ teaspoon freshly ground black pepper**
— **½ teaspoon flaky sea salt**
— **¼ teaspoon garlic powder**

1 Preheat the oven to 170°C.

2 Slice the sourdough into small cubes. Add to a bowl with the rest of the ingredients and toss everything together until the bread is coated in the oil and seasonings.

3 Put the croutons on a baking sheet and bake in the preheated oven for 8 minutes. Allow to cool – the croutons will crisp up as they cool down. Add to your favourite salad or soup or just eat them as a snack!

French Dressing

Probably the simplest of all salad dressings, French dressing is the perfect balance of sweetness and sharpness. This dressing can be used on literally any salad you choose, and even better, it only takes two minutes to make.

Serves 6 as a dressing

— 2 tablespoons white wine vinegar
— 1 tablespoon Dijon mustard
— 1 tablespoon honey
— juice of ½ small lemon
— 100ml olive oil

1 Mix all the ingredients together except the oil in a clean jam jar. Slowly drizzle in the oil, then put the lid on and give it a good shake until everything is combined.

CHEF'S NOTE: The trick to oil-based dressings is to give them a really good shake so everything emulsifies. If you make your dressing in advance, it will separate. Just give it a good shake to combine again before using.

French dressing

Classic vinaigrette

Emotional Sauce

This is basically the best burger sauce you will ever have in your life. I'm obsessed with spicy food, so I added paprika and sweet chilli sauce to give it a bit of extra heat. Try making this for your next barbecue and you'll be addicted in no time.

Serves 2 as a dip or sauce

— 1 tablespoon ketchup
— 2 tablespoons good-quality mayonnaise
— 1 gherkin, roughly chopped, plus a splash of the liquid from the gherkin jar
— 1 teaspoon brandy
— 1 stalk of fresh dill, chopped
— ½ tablespoon sweet chilli sauce
— 1 teaspoon paprika

1 Blitz all the ingredients together in a blender to form a sauce. It's really easy to scale this up if you want to make more – just double or triple everything and if you have any left over, keep it in a sealed, sterilised jar in the fridge for up to one week.

Curried Mayo

This is the ideal dip for anything crispy, golden and deep-fried. It's made for the battered sausages on page 103.

Serves 4-6 as a dip or sauce

— ½ **teaspoon garam masala**
— ½ **teaspoon paprika**
— ½ **teaspoon garlic powder**
— ½ **teaspoon ground cumin**
— ½ **teaspoon ground turmeric**
— ½ **teaspoon ground coriander**
— **100ml vegetable oil**
— **5 tablespoons good-quality mayonnaise**

1 In a frying pan, fry all the spices in the oil until fragrant and allow to cool. This is your curry oil – you can put this in a sterilised airtight jar and keep it in the cupboard for up to two weeks.

2 When you want to make up your curry mayo, just whisk 1 tablespoon of the curry oil into 5 tablespoons of mayonnaise.

CHEF'S NOTE: You can use the curry oil to make great Bombay potatoes. Just cut a couple of large potatoes into small cubes, toss in 2 tablespoons of the curry oil, then roast in the oven at 200°C for 25 minutes.

Thousand Island Dressing

There's probably a thousand different ways you can use this classic dressing, but my top three are on a crunchy green salad, with some juicy, freshly cooked prawns or smothered on a burger.

Serves 2 as a dressing

— 2 teaspoons vegetable oil
— ½ onion, diced
— 1 tablespoon good-quality mayonnaise
— 1 tablespoon tomato ketchup
— juice of ½ lemon
— 5 chives, finely chopped
— 1 teaspoon paprika
— 1 stalk of dill, finely chopped
— sea salt and freshly ground black pepper
— 1 hard-boiled egg

1 Start by softening your onion in the oil in a frying pan over a medium heat.
2 Blitz your cooked onion in a food processor with all the ingredients except the seasoning and boiled egg. Season to taste with salt and pepper, then finely grate in the egg and fold it all together.

Classic Vinaigrette

Unlike people, salads are never sexier when they're naked. Try this three-ingredient dressing next time you have a sad salad that needs a little something to dress it up.

Serves 8 as a dressing

— 2 tablespoons Dijon mustard
— 2 tablespoons balsamic vinegar
— 7 tablespoons olive oil

1 Mix the vinegar and mustard together in a clean jam jar. Drizzle in the oil, then put on the lid and shake until everything is fully combined.

Homemade Tomato Ketchup

You might think it's mad to suggest making your own ketchup, but you'll be surprised how much it can improve your basic burger.

Makes 2-3 jars

— 1 teaspoon olive oil
— ½ onion, diced
— 2 tablespoons tomato paste
— 650g fresh tomatoes, chopped
— 100g tomato passata
— 60g brown sugar
— 1 tablespoon olive oil
— 1 teaspoon ground cinnamon
— ½ teaspoon freshly grated nutmeg
— 100ml white wine vinegar
— sea salt and freshly ground black pepper

1 Heat the olive oil in a saucepan and cook the onion with the tomato paste until softened. Add the rest of the ingredients, except the seasoning, and simmer over a medium heat for 20 minutes, until well cooked and resembling a sauce. Remove from the heat and transfer to a food processor and blitz until smooth. Season to taste with salt and freshly ground black pepper.
2 To store, put the ketchup in a sterilised airtight jar and keep in the fridge for up to two weeks.

Jack Daniels BBQ sauce

Why buy a bottle of barbecue sauce when the homemade stuff is so easy to make and so much nicer? Adding Jack Daniels adds a sweet and spicy flavour without making it boozy, because all the alcohol cooks off in the pan.

Serves 6-8 as a sauce

— 200g tomato ketchup
— 3 tablespoons light brown sugar
— 2 tablespoons white wine vinegar
— 2 tablespoons Worcestershire sauce
— 3 teaspoons smoked paprika
— 100ml Jack Daniels whiskey
— 50ml honey

1 Put all the ingredients into a saucepan and bring to the boil. Reduce the heat to low and simmer, whisking regularly, until reduced and thickened. Turn off the heat and allow to cool.

2 To store, put the barbecue sauce in a sterilised airtight jar and keep in the fridge for up to two weeks.

Cucumber Raita

This is the ideal accompaniment to your favourite curry, like the chicken tikka masala on pages 150–151. It's also great served as a dip with poppadums or fresh veggies.

Serves 4 as a dip or sauce

— 200g Greek yoghurt
— 10g fresh mint leaves, finely chopped
— 10g fresh coriander leaves, finely chopped
— ½ cucumber, finely diced
— 1 teaspoon white wine vinegar
— salt and freshly ground black pepper
— fresh lemon juice, to taste

1 Place all the ingredients in a bowl and mix together. If you like a slightly smoother sauce, you can put everything in a food processer and blitz until just roughly blended. Season to taste with salt and pepper and lemon juice and serve.

Smoked Bacon Jam

This stuff just hits different. Breakfast, lunch or dinner, it's the perfect condiment for any dish. I put it on a bacon butty one day and it changed my life for the better. Try it for yourself if you don't believe me.

Makes 3-4 jars

— 220g smoked bacon, chopped
— 1 teaspoon fennel seeds
— 1 teaspoon vegetable oil
— 220g cider vinegar
— 220g tomato juice
— 20g balsamic vinegar
— 220g sugar
— 200ml black coffee
— 100g tomato paste
— 200g fresh tomatoes, chopped

1 Fry the bacon and fennel seeds in the vegetable oil in a large saucepan just until the bacon is cooked. Add in all the other ingredients and simmer for 1 hour on a low heat, stirring frequently so it doesn't burn, until it's nice and sticky. There will be a layer of fat on top of the jam but that's fine, there's no need to remove it.

2 Leave to cool, then blitz using a stick blender or in a food processor. I like to leave this with some chunks of bacon in it.

3 To store, put the jam in sterilised airtight jars and keep in the fridge for up to two weeks.

CHEF'S NOTE: Try this on sourdough toast with poached eggs, on a chicken or beef burger, or just by the spoonful!

Hollandaise Sauce

Hollandaise is the classic buttery sauce used to make eggs Benedict and it's also great on steak. It can split easily, so go nice and slow and be careful not to put it on a direct heat.

Serves 4-6 as a sauce

— 280g unsalted butter
— 4 egg yolks
— 35ml white wine vinegar
— a pinch of salt
— juice of ¼ lemon

1 Start by clarifying your butter. To do this, melt the butter over a very low heat in a small saucepan. The milk solids will rise to the top of the butter as it melts – they're foamy and white.

2 Once the butter is completed melted, take it off the heat. Skim the milk solids from the top of the butterfat using a ladle or slotted spoon and discard them. Next, ladle the butterfat from the saucepan into a jug or bowl. There will be a white, milky substance in the bottom of the saucepan – discard this. You now have clarified butter.

3 To make the hollandaise, put the egg yolks and vinegar in a metal bowl and whisk well until fluffy.

4 Set the bowl over a pot of barely simmering water, not allowing the bottom of the bowl to touch the water. Add in the clarified butter very slowly while whisking constantly. When all the butter has been added, the sauce should be light and fluffy and should coat the back of a spoon. Finish by whisking in the salt and lemon juice.

CHEF'S NOTE: If you're making hollandaise sauce, you just have to make eggs Benedict. Split and toast two English muffins, then top each muffin half with a slice of cooked bacon, a poached egg and a generous pour of hollandaise sauce.

Adding a tablespoon of chopped fresh tarragon at the end turns this into Béarnaise sauce, which is amazing over steak.

Basil Oil

If you like pesto, you'll love this. It's great as a salad dressing, drizzled over buttered pasta or as a finishing touch for any chicken or steak dish.

Makes 1 jar

— 2 big bunches of fresh basil
— 300ml vegetable oil

1 Bring a pot of water to the boil and fill a bowl with water and a handful of ice cubes. Carefully place the basil into the boiling water. In a few seconds the basil will wilt – immediately remove it with a slotted spoon to the ice water and allow to cool.
2 Squeeze the water out of the basil using a clean kitchen towel, then blitz the basil with the oil in a food processor. Stain to remove any larger pieces of basil.
3 To store, put the basil oil in a sterilised airtight jar and keep in the cupboard for up to two weeks.

CHEF'S NOTE: Make sure to squeeze as much water as possible out of your basil to prevent any water droplets from getting into the oil.

ACKNOWLEDGMENTS

I would firstly like to thank everyone who has supported me on TikTok and Instagram. Anyone who has liked, shared or posted nice comments, and of course my food sponsors – just know that I love you all. I am now able to call this my job, and that really is a dream come true.

To TikTok, for giving me a platform to express my views on food and create recipes for the whole world to follow.

To my nana, for getting me my first chef job in a kitchen, and for always supporting my dreams. To Crea and Carey, for your endless support, advice and guidance, it really is much appreciated. You have always supported and guided me in the right direction.

To Demeter and Jules, for spotting my talent very early on, and for taking a chance on little old me. I couldn't have asked for better agents and I couldn't have done this without you both.

To everyone at HarperCollins Ireland. I still remember the day Jules and Demeter rang me and told me that Catherine from HarperCollins Ireland wanted to publish my book. I nearly passed out with excitement! So to Catherine, thank you so much for making my dream come true. And to Kerri, for the long days and hours spent helping me write this book, it really helped that you were on Masterchef! You really know your stuff and your passion for food was very easy to see.

To Charlotte, Leo and Clare, for teaching me so much about styling and photographing food. It was a pleasure to work with you.

And finally, thanks to my haters ... you really fuelled me to push myself even more.

INDEX